Medical Marijuana

by Kevin Hillstrom

LUCENT BOOKS

A part of Gale, Cengage Learning

GALE
CENGAGE Learning·

Farmington Hills, Mich • San Francisco • New York • Waterville, Maine
Meriden, Conn • Mason, Ohio • Chicago

B

© 2014 Gale, Cengage Learning

WCN:01-100-101

LIBRARY OF CONGRESS CATALOGING-IN-PUBLICATION DATA

Hillstrom, Kevin, 1963- author.
  Medical marijuana / by Kevin Hillstrom.
    pages cm. -- (Hot topics)
  Audience: 10-13.
   Summary: "The books in this series objectively and thoughtfully explore topics of political, social, cultural, economic, moral, historical, or environmental importance"-- Provided by publisher.
  Includes bibliographical references and index.
   ISBN 978-1-4205-0871-0 (hardback)
  1. Marijuana--Therapeutic use--Juvenile literature. I. Title.
  RM666.C266H55 2014
  615.7'827--dc 3
                                                                2014003364

Lucent Books
27500 Drake Rd.
Farmington Hills, MI 48331

ISBN-13: 978-1-4205-0871-0
ISBN-10: 1-4205-0871-7

Printed in the United States of America
1 2 3 4 5 6 7 18 17 16 15 14

CONTENTS

FOREWORD

Young people today are bombarded with information. Aside from traditional sources such as newspapers, television, and the radio, they are inundated with a nearly continuous stream of data from electronic media. They send and receive e-mails and instant messages, read and write online "blogs," participate in chat rooms and forums, and surf the web for hours. This trend is likely to continue. As Patricia Senn Breivik, the former dean of university libraries at Wayne State University in Detroit, has stated, "Information overload will only increase in the future. By 2020, for example, the available body of information is expected to double every 73 days! How will these students find the information they need in this coming tidal wave of information?"

Ironically, this overabundance of information can actually impede efforts to understand complex issues. Whether the topic is abortion, the death penalty, gay rights, or obesity, the deluge of fact and opinion that floods the print and electronic media is overwhelming. The news media report the results of polls and studies that contradict one another. Cable news shows, talk radio programs, and newspaper editorials promote narrow viewpoints and omit facts that challenge their own political biases. The World Wide Web is an electronic minefield where legitimate scholars compete with the postings of ordinary citizens who may or may not be well-informed or capable of reasoned argument. At times, strongly worded testimonials and opinion pieces both in print and electronic media are presented as factual accounts.

Conflicting quotes and statistics can confuse even the most diligent researchers. A good example of this is the question of whether or not the death penalty deters crime. For instance, one study found that murders decreased by nearly one-third when the death penalty was reinstated in New York in 1995. Death penalty supporters cite this finding to support their argument that the existence of the death penalty deters criminals from committing murder. However, another study found that states without the death penalty have murder rates below the national average. This study is cited by opponents of capital punishment,

he death penalty deters murder. Stu-
ar, informed discussion if they are to
nformed decisions.

; designed to help young people wade
pinion, and rhetoric so that they can
roversial issues. Only by reading and
be able to formulate a viewpoint that
views of others. Each volume of the
day's most pressing social issues and
ew of the topic. Carefully crafted nar-
rimary and secondary source quotes,
study questions all provide excellent
h and discussion. Full-color photo-
 all volumes in the series. With its
ot Topics series is a valuable resource
 to understand the pressing issues of

INTRODUCTION

THE DEBATE OVER MEDICAL MARIJUANA

For much of the twentieth century, most Americans viewed marijuana as a dangerous and destructive drug. They dismissed marijuana smokers as unmotivated "stoners" and saw marijuana use as a pathway to extremely addictive illicit drugs like heroin and cocaine. In the 1960s and 1970s, though, public perceptions of marijuana began to change. This shift was driven in part by changing cultural attitudes, but it was also fed by reports from scientists and marijuana users that the marijuana plant had significant medicinal qualities.

"Medical marijuana" has since emerged as one of the most intensely debated issues in American society. Supporters of total marijuana legalization have seized on the plant's alleged health benefits as a weapon in their crusade. Meanwhile, critics opposed to legalization have attacked reports of marijuana's therapeutic properties. They claim that these reports are flawed or fail to account for marijuana's negative impact on families and communities.

Today Americans seeking to educate themselves about the alleged perils and benefits of medical marijuana hear dramatically different descriptions of the drug. "Both those who advocate and those who oppose the medical use of marijuana claim to have science on their side," states the Institute of Medicine, the chief advisory body to the U.S. government on health and medical issues. "Each camp selectively cites research that supports its position, and each occasionally misrepresents study findings. . . . At times advocates for medical marijuana have appeared to be discussing a different drug than their opponents."[1]

For many years the battle over medical marijuana proceeded with neither side gaining a firm advantage. In the early twenty-first century, however, supporters of medical marijuana won a series of important victories in state-level ballot initiatives. By the close of the 2012 election season, eighteen states and the District of Columbia had legalized medical marijuana prescriptions to help patients cope with various ailments and diseases. Medical marijuana advocates are now convinced that the plant will eventually be accepted nationally as a legitimate patient-care tool. Opponents, however, vow to continue warning the public about the underappreciated dangers of medical marijuana.

THE HISTORY OF MEDICAL MARIJUANA

The cannabis plant, also commonly known as marijuana, has been used for medicinal purposes by civilizations around the world for centuries. Historians say that the herb was used as a remedy for health ailments at least as far back as 2700 B.C., when Chinese emperor Shun Nung mentioned it in an ancient medical text called *Pen Ts'ao*. As time passed, Chinese physicians became increasingly familiar with the plant's properties and its effects on the human body. They discovered, for example, that cannabis flowers and leaves contain material capable of altering bodily sensations and brain activity. Modern-day scientists have identified the main chemical compound responsible for these temporary sensations—now commonly known as getting high—as tetrahydrocannabinol, or THC.

The ancient Chinese eventually adopted cannabis as a preferred medicine for a wide range of health problems, including malaria, constipation, and joint pain. The Chinese also developed different ways of delivering cannabis to patients, including teas, salves, and ointments. Historians report that by A.D. 220, it was even being used in China as a surgical anesthetic.

Cannabis was not employed solely for medical purposes, though. The ancient Chinese made sophisticated use of another variety of the cannabis plant known as hemp. This cultivated strain of cannabis was characterized by strong and hardy stalk fibers and low concentrations of THC. The Chinese used hemp to make rope, sails, clothing, paper, and other materials.

Cannabis Spreads Across Asia, the Middle East, and Africa

Cannabis cultivation spread from China into other parts of Asia, including Japan, Korea, and India. The herb made a particularly big impact on ancient India, where people not only made heavy use of hemp but also embraced the psychoactive (mind-altering) properties of cannabis strains with high THC content. By 1400 B.C. marijuana had been absorbed into Indian spiritual and religious rites because of its usefulness in delivering what one ancient text called "freedom from distress."[2] Over time it also became a common treatment for hundreds of different health problems.

The introduction of cannabis into the eastern expanses of Asia (modern-day Russia) and the Middle East has been attributed to tribes of nomadic horsemen, known collectively as Scythians, who once lived along the eastern borderlands of China's ancient kingdoms. The Scythians used cannabis-based vapor baths for the purposes of intoxication, but they also used the plant to treat illness and in their burial rituals.

As the Scythians moved eastward, they brought cannabis to ancient Mesopotamian civilizations. Medical practitioners in ancient Egypt used cannabis to treat a wide array of health problems, from hemorrhoids to failing eyesight. Scholar Michael Aldrich writes that health-care practitioners in the empire of Assyria (in modern-day northern Iraq) may have used cannabis "externally as a bandage and in salves for swellings and bruises, and internally for depression of spirits, impotence, 'poison of all limbs' (arthritis?), kidney stones, for a 'female ailment,' and for the annulment of witchcraft."[3] Historians also believe that Arab traders of the Middle Ages introduced cannabis to eastern African kingdoms.

Ancient Greeks and Romans also incorporated marijuana into their medical care, using it to treat earaches, inflammation, joint pain, and other problems. The famous Roman physician, surgeon, and philosopher Galen, who lived and practiced in the second century A.D., emphasized the power of cannabis to affect the mind and body when consumed orally: "Cooked and

The Greek historian Herodotus wrote about the Scythians' use of the wild hemp plant in his history of the Persian wars.

consumed with dessert after dinner, it stimulates the appetite for drinking, and in excess sends a warm and toxic vapor to the head."[4]

From Europe to the New World

In the cooler climates of western and northern Europe, cannabis plants with high levels of THC did not grow very well. The variety of cannabis known as hemp, however, could be cultivated in European soil and weather. First introduced into this region in the Middle Ages, hemp evolved into a crucial resource for Europe's major seafaring powers. The great Dutch, English, French, Portuguese, and Spanish fleets that plied the world's oceans during this era were all outfitted with ropes, netting, and sails made of saltwater-resistant hemp.

Hemp was used in Europe during the 1500s and 1600s to produce a great variety of other items, from cloth to writing paper to paint canvases. It also became an ingredient in European folk remedies, even though it did not contain the high levels of THC found in marijuana grown in warmer parts of the world. Despite the fact that it did not "deliver much by way of euphoria," writes historian Martin A. Lee, "hemp served as a multipurpose medicine—for quelling fevers, soothing burns, relieving headaches, and dressing wounds with a disinfectant paste made of hemp flowers, wax, and olive oil."[5]

Cannabis came to the Americas in the sixteenth century, when slave ships of the Spanish and Portuguese empires began supplying labor for sugar plantations in the New World. Some of the African slaves forced to work in these outposts, which lay scattered across the Caribbean and modern-day Brazil, brought cannabis seeds with them. Cannabis cultivation gradually took root on several of these plantations, as overseers and administrators recognized the profits they could reap by diversifying into hemp production. But cannabis also came to be prized by South American native peoples. Following the lead of African slave laborers, they began to use marijuana for both medical and recreational purposes. Many Indians who already used psychoactive plants in their religious rites and ceremonies also incorporated marijuana into their spiritual lives.

Cannabis in the Early United States

Hemp cultivation slowly trickled northward into colonial America. As in Europe, hemp was highly valued in the colonies as material for rope, cloth, canvas sails, and paper. The first American flags were even made of hemp cloth. Hemp production expanded further in the early 1800s as American pioneers pushed westward into the interior of the North American continent. By

ROPE-MAKERS

A nineteenth-century hemp-rope-making machine from colonial America. Hemp production expanded in the early 1800s as American pioneers pushed farther westward across the continent.

the mid-nineteenth century, hemp was the nation's third-largest crop, behind only cotton and tobacco.

Use of cannabis for medical purposes in the United States, however, remained virtually nonexistent until the mid-nineteenth century. At that time doctors in the United States, Canada, and Europe built upon groundbreaking research conducted several years earlier by an Irish physician named William O'Shaughnessy. During the 1830s O'Shaughnessy served as a physician with the British East India Company in India. He became fascinated by the natives' use of cannabis to treat sickness. The Irish doctor subsequently conducted his own experiments with cannabis. He concluded that the plant really was effective in treating muscle spasms, digestive problems, pain, and other afflictions. When O'Shaughnessy published his findings in 1841, other Western physicians and medical researchers began to carry out their own cannabis studies.

Cannabis Goes Mainstream

Interest in cannabis for therapeutic purposes intensified in the United States in the mid-1800s. In 1860 the Ohio State Medical Society conducted the first official U.S. government study of what is now known as medical marijuana. The organization reported that, according to its review of historical medical records, certain strains of cannabis were effective in relieving a wide variety of health problems, from respiratory ailments to postpartum depression. Other physicians and researchers endorsed the therapeutic properties of the plant as well. "No less a figure than Sir William Osler, often called the founder of modern medicine, endorsed cannabis as the best treatment for migraine headaches,"[6] writes Lee.

By the 1880s and 1890s, cannabis had become an important ingredient in hundreds of patent medicines sold in the United States. Patent medicines were unregulated drug compounds that were touted as cures for virtually every conceivable illness or physical problem seen in American households. Since no restrictions existed in America during this era regarding the manufacture, promotion, sale, or purchase of medicine, the marketplace was full of products that were either worthless or actually dangerous to use. Other medicines of this period, however, were based on traditional folk remedies that used cannabis and other plants with legitimate medicinal properties.

During this same time a small but growing number of Americans started consuming cannabis strictly for recreational purposes—that is, as a means of relaxing and socializing with friends. By the late 1880s nearly every big American city supported one or more establishments known as hash dens (hashish is a potent extract of cannabis). Users of cannabis and hashish also switched from eating the substances to smoking them. This change, explains Lee, "was partly attributable to the belated realization that they could achieve a milder, quicker, and more manageable high by inhaling cannabis fumes instead of guzzling a tincture [a liquid extract] or chewing a pastry."[7]

The Tide Turns Against Cannabis

At the beginning of the twentieth century, cannabis did not have a particularly dark or unsavory reputation in the United States. Over the next few decades, however, the plant was unceremoniously pushed to the margins of American medicine and society. This shift resulted from a long power struggle that pitted people who wanted to keep American health care unregulated against practitioners of "regular" medicine.

The so-called Regulars were professionally trained and formally educated physicians, surgeons, and pharmacists who wanted to impose new training and licensing requirements for health-care providers. For example, they urged the government to close hundreds of medical schools that were willing to hand out diplomas to anyone who could pay for one, regardless of skill or knowledge. The Regulars' crusade was driven partly by the desire to reduce the number of practicing doctors and therapists so that they could claim more patients for themselves. But it also stemmed from a genuine desire to improve the quality of medical care across the nation.

A SAFE AND EFFECTIVE DRUG

"The evidence . . . clearly shows that marijuana has been accepted as capable of relieving the distress of great numbers of very ill people. . . . Marijuana in its natural form is one of the safest therapeutically active substances known to man."—DEA judge Francis Young in 1988

Quoted in Rudolph Joseph Gerber. *Legalizing Marijuana: Drug Policy Reform and Prohibition Politics.* Westport, CT: Greenwood, 2004, p. 102.

By 1915 or so, the Regulars had largely won the battle to regulate American health care. Specialists in herbal medicine—including many who used cannabis in their treatments—were driven out of business by new laws and regulations. One of the most important of these new laws was the 1906 Pure Food and Drug Act, which was crafted specifically to improve the safety of American drugs and get dangerous patent medicines off market shelves. This federal legislation, which established the U.S. government as a watchdog over all drugs sold in the country, was the first to mention cannabis. The act did not forbid its use, but it included the plant among a list of intoxicants that had to be identified on drug labels when used as an ingredient.

Around this same time, several towns and states in the American Southwest outlawed the possession, sale, or use of

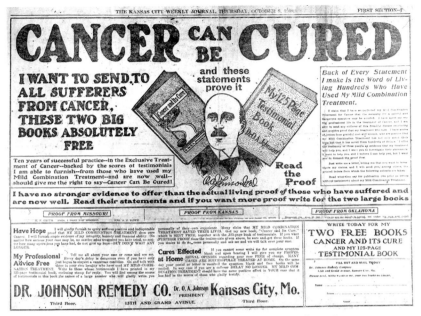

The 1906 Food and Drug Act was crafted to improve the safety of American drugs and get dangerous patent medicines and quack remedies such as the one advertised here off market shelves. It also listed marijuana as an intoxicant.

cannabis. Historians assert that the main purpose of these laws was to harass newly arrived Mexican immigrants. Thousands of Mexicans had poured into America's border states in the first two decades of the twentieth century, fleeing civil war and economic depression in their homeland. By the late 1910s many whites in California and Texas in particular had grown resentful of these outsiders. They viewed the immigrants as intellectually and morally inferior—and as potential threats to their jobs. Laws that outlawed cannabis, which many Mexican laborers enjoyed smoking after working in the fields all day, became a way for whites to show the immigrants that they were not welcome.

An Intensifying Crusade Against Marijuana

The reputation of cannabis went into an even steeper tailspin during the 1920s and 1930s. This decline was partly due to the religious and moral convictions of millions of Americans who felt that alcohol and mind-altering drugs were sinful and contributed to poverty, domestic violence, and many other social problems. These beliefs also paved the way for Prohibition, a thirteen-year period (1920 to 1933) in which alcoholic beverages were outlawed across America.

American attitudes about marijuana also were influenced by laws against cannabis that were passed by other nations. Both Canada and the United Kingdom passed laws prohibiting the possession or use of cannabis in the 1920s. These laws were designed mostly to curb the use of addictive drugs like opium, morphine, and cocaine. When cannabis was added to the mix of prohibited drugs, though, the plant's reputation suffered further damage.

Hemp's declining commercial importance also hurt the cannabis cause. By the early 1900s the cotton gin and other industrial innovations had made cotton the primary material in the production of clothing, blankets, pillowcases, and other goods. Hemp was largely forgotten. When hemp ceased to be a major economic resource, defenders of cannabis lost one of their main arguments for cultivation of the plant.

Racism and cultural bias also remained a key factor in cannabis's sagging fortunes in the United States. During the 1920s the practice of smoking cannabis—or marijuana, as it was called by Spanish-speaking Mexicans—was closely associated with Mexican immigrants and black jazz musicians in New York and other big cities.

For a nation that was largely rural and white in the early twentieth century, these associations deepened the feeling that smoking marijuana was a strange and alien practice. By 1931 twenty-nine states had criminalized the possession, sale, or use of marijuana within their borders.

"The Hideous Monster Marihuana"

Concerns about marijuana were further heightened by newspapers and federal authorities. One of the plant's biggest critics was the famed newspaper baron William Randolph Hearst, and the papers in his empire regularly spoke out against the drug. "Marijuana is a shortcut to the insane asylum,"[8] warned Hearst's *San Francisco Examiner* in 1923.

Harry Anslinger was appointed the first commissioner of the U.S. Treasury Department's Federal Bureau of Narcotics in 1930. In his thirty-two-year tenure he sought long prison sentences for anyone caught selling or possessing marijuana.

The man most responsible for turning cannabis into a drug that struck terror in the hearts of American parents and community leaders, however, was Harry Anslinger. He was appointed as the first commissioner of the U.S. Treasury Department's Federal Bureau of Narcotics. Anslinger received this appointment in August 1930, and he directed the bureau for the next thirty-two years. During that time he sought long prison sentences for anyone caught selling or possessing marijuana. He also repeatedly described marijuana in the most frightening terms. "It is a drug that causes insanity, criminality, and death—the most violence-causing drug in the history of mankind,"[9] insisted Anslinger. In 1937 he declared that "if the hideous monster Frankenstein came face-to-face with the hideous monster Marihuana [an alternate spelling common in the early 1900s], he would drop dead of fright."[10]

These sorts of statements troubled the American Medical Association (AMA), the nation's leading organization of physicians. When Congress considered passing a tax on marijuana that would make it difficult to study its medical usefulness, the AMA's top lawyer, William Woodward, urged the lawmakers to reconsider. "To say . . . that the use of the drug should be prevented by a prohibitive tax, loses sight of the fact that future investigation may show that there are substantial medical uses for cannabis,"[11] he stated.

Despite Woodward's protest, Congress passed the Marihuana Tax Act in 1937. This law made criminals of anyone who possessed the drug, failed to pay a steep tax based on the quantity they held, and used marijuana for anything other than a few carefully defined medical or industrial purposes. Four years later all forms of cannabis were removed from the *U.S. Pharmacopeia National Formulary*, a guidebook of standards for the production of pharmaceutical drugs, food ingredients, and dietary supplements.

Marijuana Proponents Fight Back

For much of the 1940s and 1950s, most Americans held the view that marijuana was a dangerous drug with no redeeming value. This stance was reflected in the enactment of new federal laws such as the 1951 Boggs Act and the 1956 Narcotics Control Act, which established mandatory sentences for trafficking, possession, or use of marijuana, cocaine, heroin, and other narcotics. After these measures became law, an individual convicted on a first-offense marijuana-possession charge could face a prison sentence of two to ten years and a fine of up to twenty thousand dollars. These laws drove recreational marijuana use further underground, but they failed to eradicate it altogether.

U.S. research into possible medical uses for marijuana virtually disappeared during this period. Overseas, however, medical researchers made important discoveries about cannabis. Several studies released during the 1960s suggested that the drug might be helpful in treating glaucoma, a leading cause of blindness. In 1964 Israeli scientist Raphael Mechoulam produced a synthetic (human-created) version of THC, the main psychoactive ingredient in marijuana. This discovery delighted researchers who wanted to study THC's potential therapeutic properties without worrying about marijuana's legal status.

CONFUSING RULES FOR MARIJUANA

"In a short time, pot has gone from being a prohibited substance to one that is, in many places, widely available if you have an ache or a pain and the patience to fuss with a few forms. . . . And so what is emerging in many places is a strange, bipolar set of rules: dope is forbidden for everyone but totally O.K. for anyone who is willing to claim a chronic muscle spasm. Does anyone take such farcical distinctions seriously?"—Journalist Andrew Ferguson

Andrew Ferguson. "The United States of Amerijuana." *Time*, November 11, 2010. www
.time.com/time/magazine/article/0,9171,2030925,00.html.

Other scientists, meanwhile, continued to focus their energies on the cannabis plant and its many natural chemical components. Evidence of marijuana's therapeutic properties continued to pile up in the early 1970s. Scientists reported that the plant could help reduce clinical depression, aid in organ transplant procedures, and reduce nausea and vomiting in cancer patients undergoing chemotherapy.

Growing excitement about marijuana in America's medical and scientific communities was overshadowed, though, by a sudden explosion of recreational marijuana use in white communities across the United States. This surge in the use of marijuana began in the 1950s with the beat generation, the name given to some young Americans who consciously rebelled

The Rosa Parks of Medical Marijuana

In 1976 a young college professor named Robert C. Randall successfully sued the federal government for the right to smoke marijuana. Randall had discovered over the space of several years that smoking cannabis could control his glaucoma, which otherwise would have rendered him blind. When he was arrested for marijuana possession, the courts accepted Randall's argument that it had been necessary for him to break the law in order to save his eyesight. The federal government subsequently agreed to provide Randall with marijuana from a special experimental cannabis farm in Mississippi that it had maintained since 1968 (this production facility was established to provide scientific researchers with a legal source of marijuana).

Admirers have compared Randall's defiance of federal medical marijuana laws to civil rights icon Rosa Parks's rebellion against segregationist laws in the South. Journalist Martin A. Lee notes that Randall's stand ultimately "compelled the Food and Drug Administration to establish a special Compassionate Investigational New Drug Program, whereby desperately ill patients, if they were very persistent and lucky, could gain access to government-grown cannabis. For twenty-five years until his untimely death in 2001, Randall smoked ten legal marijuana cigarettes a day. And he never went blind."

Martin A. Lee. *Smoke Signals: A Social History of Marijuana—Medical, Recreational, and Scientific.* New York: Scribner, 2012, pp. 142–143.

against what they saw as an overly restrictive and materialistic culture in America. This turn to marijuana—as well as more potent drugs like LSD and heroin—intensified in the 1960s, when America was rocked by serious divisions over civil rights, the Vietnam War, sexual freedom, environmental pollution, and other issues.

Many of these divisions broke down over generational lines, as young people of every race searched for ways to show their unhappiness with the society that awaited them in adulthood. They marched against the war and for civil rights and adopted hippie clothing and hairstyles. Many of them also became attracted to marijuana, not only because they enjoyed getting high but also because the illegal activity made conservative, older Americans so angry. "Marijuana prohibition became self-perpetuating," writes journalist Jacob Sullum. "The sort of people who were eager to use it as a sign of rebellion disgusted the sort of people who were determined to keep it illegal."[12]

Medical Marijuana and the Controlled Substances Act

During the 1970s and 1980s, opposition to recreational use of marijuana softened across much of the United States; however, opposition to marijuana use remained strong in many households and communities. But other Americans came to feel that smoking pot (a common nickname for marijuana) was not a big deal. These shifting attitudes were partly due to the fact that marijuana use infiltrated middle-class white, black, and Hispanic families and neighborhoods. Another factor was that American popular culture—novels, music, and movies—increasingly treated marijuana as a harmless pleasure, not a pathway to misery. By the end of the 1970s, several states had even passed laws eliminating criminal penalties for marijuana possession and use. In addition, the National Organization for the Reform of Marijuana Laws, or NORML (founded in 1970), had become a nationally known lobbying organization for the decriminalization of pot.

From 1978 to 1982 thirty-three states also passed bills that either supported medical research on marijuana or approved limited medicinal use of marijuana. Calls for new marijuana research were thwarted, however, by the 1970 Controlled Substances Act (CSA), which was part of the Comprehensive Drug Abuse Prevention and Control Act of 1970. "This law superseded all prior federal drug statutes and classified most drugs within one of five different schedules based on their safety, medicinal value, and risks of abuse," explain scholars Wendy Chapkis and Richard J. Webb. "Under the CSA, marijuana—like heroin and LSD—is classified as a Schedule 1 controlled substance, meaning that it has no currently accepted medical use, a high potential for abuse, and is unsafe even if used under a doctor's supervision."[13] This classification made it much more difficult for U.S.

scientists to obtain funding and other support for research into marijuana's potential medical benefits.

Marijuana legalization efforts made little headway in the 1980s, which featured strong Just Say No antidrug campaigns crafted by Republican president Ronald Reagan and other conservative politicians. In the 1990s, NORML and other advocates for the full legalization of marijuana decided to focus their time and resources on the medical marijuana issue. "If we get medical access, we're going to get legalization eventually," activist Richard Cowan said in 1993. "The cat will be out of the bag."[14] Mindful that medical marijuana enjoyed more support from the general public than from elected lawmakers, advocates pushed to get medical marijuana referenda on state ballots.

Pro-medical-marijuana forces secured their first big victory in 1996 when voters in California passed Proposition 215, which legalized medical cannabis use, possession, and cultivation. Three years later activists received a big boost from the Institute of Medicine, the official advisory group on health-care science to the U.S. government. The institute stated in a widely publicized study that scientific research "indicate[s] a potential therapeutic value for cannabinoid drugs [drugs derived from cannabis], particularly for symptoms such as pain relief, control of nausea and vomiting, and appetite stimulation."[15] By the end of 2000, residents of the District of Columbia and seven more states (Alaska, Arizona, Colorado, Maine, Nevada, Oregon, and Washington) had all voted to legalize medical marijuana, despite continued opposition from the federal government. In 2000 Hawaii's state legislature became the nation's first to pass medical cannabis legislation.

Opponents of marijuana legalization have acknowledged that the pro-pot camp made a smart strategic decision in pushing state-level medical marijuana measures. As journalist Matt Labash writes, "Turns out—no surprise—when you ask people if their fellow citizens dying of cancer-AIDS should be allowed to have a puff or two during their last moments, most Americans say sure, why not?"[16]

*A woman receives medical marijuana through a buyer's club in California.
In 1996 voters in California passed Proposition 215, which legalized medical
cannabis use, possession, and cultivation.*

New Battlegrounds Open Up

Confrontations over medical marijuana further intensified in
the first decade of the twenty-first century. Other states stepped
forward to defy the federal government's prohibitions against
the possession, sale, or use of marijuana for medical purposes.
From 2004 through 2010 voters in Montana (2004), Michigan
(2008), and Arizona (2010) all approved medical marijuana ballot measures. State legislatures in Vermont (2004), Rhode Is-
land (2006), New Mexico (2007), and New Jersey (2010) passed
medical cannabis legislation as well.

The battle over medical marijuana also spilled again and again into the nation's courts, with both sides claiming significant victories. In 2005, for example, the antilegalization camp rejoiced when the U.S. Supreme Court ruled in *Gonzales v. Raich* that the federal government had the authority to criminalize the production and use of homegrown medical marijuana in states that had approved the plant's use for medicinal purposes.

Two years later, however, pro-medical-pot forces celebrated when Colorado courts greatly expanded the number of patients that state medical marijuana growers could keep as clients. This ruling produced a flood of new businesses, commonly known as dispensaries, to meet the rising demand for medicinal cannabis. In the two years after the ruling, notes *Time*, "more than 1,000 dispensaries sprang up to serve the more than 100,000 Coloradans who had suddenly discovered their need for medical marijuana and applied for a patient card. As [comedian and political commentator] Jon Stewart noted, what had been considered the healthiest state in the country rapidly became one of the sickest."[17]

Mixed Signals and Mass Confusion

Since that time, medical marijuana has been on an unpredictable roller-coaster ride. In 2011 lawmakers in Delaware passed a medical marijuana legalization law on the same day that Maryland's governor signed a bill protecting medical marijuana users from arrest. One year later voters in Massachusetts legalized the medical use of marijuana (becoming the seventeenth state to do so), and voters in Colorado and Washington approved ballot initiatives legalizing marijuana not just for medical purposes, but for recreational use.

Opponents of medicinal cannabis legislation point out, however, that the federal Controlled Substances Act still has more legal weight and authority than any state law. The Controlled Substances Act continues to regard all use and trade of marijuana to be a criminal act. Antipot activists have also been encouraged by several blows to the medical marijuana movement. These have ranged from failures to get legalization initiatives on state ballots to a 2012 decision by the Los Angeles City Council to greatly reduce the number of licensed medical marijuana dispensaries across the city. In February 2013, meanwhile, the Michigan Supreme Court ruled that local communities in the state had the authority to outlaw medical marijuana dispensaries as a public nuisance.

These recent skirmishes in the medical marijuana wars underscore important differences in medical cannabis laws from state to state. Author Greg Campbell explains:

> What the authors of such measures deemed to be [acceptable] to voters in California, for example, varies from what backers thought they would approve in Montana or Maine or New Mexico. The result is a confusing set of regulations from state to state that vary in the number of plants one can grow, the requirements for applying as a medical marijuana patient, how and under what circumstances a person can sell pot to others, and even the types of ailments that qualify one as a medical pot smoker."[18]

Despite state laws legalizing the medical use of marijuana, the Federal Controlled Substances Act continues to regard all use and trade of the plant to be a criminal act.

A Ninety-Three-Year Prison Sentence for Growing Medical Marijuana

In the mid-1990s an Oklahoma computer programmer and father of two named Will Foster discovered that marijuana helped ease the pain of his arthritis. He began growing marijuana in his home for his own personal use. On December 28, 1995, however, police raided his home and arrested him for his marijuana operation. He was found guilty of growing marijuana with the intent to distribute and sentenced to ninety-three years in prison.

Thanks in part to legal efforts by medical marijuana advocates, Foster's sentence was reduced to twenty years in 1998. In 2001 he was released from prison on parole and moved to California, where he could legally grow medical marijuana for himself. In 2008, though, police again arrested him for maintaining an illegal growing operation. Foster spent the next year in jail before law enforcement officials finally admitted that he had not broken any state laws. At that point, though, Oklahoma officials decided that Foster's marijuana-growing activities constituted a violation of his parole. They demanded that Foster go back into their prison system and complete his twenty-year sentence. He spent a year in jail before the Oklahoma parole board decided that Foster had not actually violated his parole. In November 2009 Oklahoma governor Brad Henry granted Foster his release, allowing him to return to his family in California.

Another big area of uncertainty concerns the posture of federal lawmakers and officials toward medical marijuana. When Democratic nominee Barack Obama was elected president in November 2008, medical marijuana advocates speculated that the federal government might adopt a more friendly stance toward medicinal cannabis legalization. Obama acknowledged on many occasions that he had smoked pot as a young man. During the presidential campaign he also stated, "I would not have the Justice Department prosecuting and raiding medical marijuana users. It's not a good use of our resources."[19]

In October 2009 Obama's Justice Department issued a memorandum to federal prosecutors advising them to make medical marijuana a low priority in their law enforcement efforts. In

2010, however, Obama nominated Michele Leonhart to head the Drug Enforcement Administration (DEA). A well-known critic of medical marijuana, Leonhart had served since 2007 as acting administrator of the DEA. Leonhart's nomination—and her confirmation by the U.S. Senate in the fall of 2010—was widely interpreted as a threat to medical marijuana legalization efforts. Also in 2010, the DEA conducted a series of highly publicized raids on medical marijuana dispensaries in Nevada, Michigan, and California. The agency said that the raids were warranted because the dispensaries were openly engaging in illicit drug dealing.

In 2011 the Justice Department issued yet another memo that encouraged federal prosecutors in states across the country to actively investigate dispensaries and other participants in the medical marijuana industry, especially if they seemed to be making lots of money. "Persons who are in the business of cultivating, selling or distributing marijuana . . . are in violation of the Controlled Substances Act, regardless of state law," the memo stated, adding, "The Department of Justice is committed to the enforcement of the Controlled Substances Act in all States."[20] According to the *Economist*, "The overall effect [of the 2011 memo] has been to confuse everybody and leave matters entirely at the discretion of individual prosecutors."[21]

How Medical Marijuana Works

Over the last half century, scientists and doctors have gained important insights into the cannabis plant. They have gained a deeper understanding of the main chemicals that give the plant its psychoactive properties and the effects that those chemical compounds have on the human body. Researchers say, however, that some people involved in the fight over legalizing marijuana for medical purposes try to twist these basic scientific facts to support their own views. In a prominent 1999 report titled *Marijuana and Medicine*, the Institute of Medicine stated:

> Both those who advocate and those who oppose the medical use of marijuana claim to have science on their side. Each camp selectively cites research that supports its position, and each occasionally misrepresents study findings. Unfortunately, these skewed interpretations have frequently served as the main source of scientific information on the subject. . . . But the public controversy over the medical use of marijuana does not reflect scientific controversy. Scientists who study marijuana and its effects on the human body largely agree about the risks posed by its use as well as the potential benefits it may provide.[22]

These insights into the effects of marijuana on the human body are based on scientific documentation of the cannabis plant itself, as well as studies of the many chemical compounds that are present in its flowers, leaves, stems, and seeds.

Two Main Types of Medical Cannabis

Two different species of the cannabis plant—*Cannabis sativa* and *Cannabis indica*—account for virtually all of the marijuana that is cultivated for medical or recreational use. *Cannabis sativa* plants can reach heights of 20 feet (6m) or so when mature,

Cannabis sativa *(shown) is one species of marijuana used for medicinal purposes.*

and they feature long, thin leaves. The near-simultaneous growing and flowering period for pure strains of *Cannabis sativa* is about six months; it is this flowering stage that produces the chemical-drenched buds that are harvested for consumption. Once the buds have been picked, they are dried so that they can be smoked or ingested orally—usually as an ingredient in tea, brownies, or some other food.

Cannabis indica plants are shorter than their *Cannabis sativa* cousins, rarely exceeding 6 feet (1.8m) in height. They also have a denser, bushlike appearance due to their thick foliage, which is composed of broad, dark-green leaves. The growing and flowering periods for *Cannabis indica* plants are more distinct than for *Cannabis sativa* plants. *Cannabis indica* buds are usually harvested six to eight weeks after flowering begins.

People who use cannabis for medicinal purposes select from these two varieties, depending on their individual needs. Golden State Collective Cannabis Laboratories, which provides chemical analysis of marijuana strains offered by California dispensaries, explains:

> Sativa strains produce more of a euphoric high, lifting the consumer's mood and therapeutically relieving stress. Indica strains relax muscle and work as general analgesics [pain relievers], also helping with sleep. A cancer patient hoping to relieve the pain from chemotherapy would benefit greatly from the effects of an Indica plant bud, whereas an individual dealing with depression would better benefit from a Sativa plant bud.[23]

Medical marijuana products usually come from various hybrids of these two types of cannabis. These hybrids not only grow more quickly than pure strains of *Cannabis sativa*, they are also bred to address specific ailments (in the case of medical marijuana) or to produce different physical and emotional sensations (in the case of recreational pot).

The Cannabis indica *plant (shown) is shorter and more broad-leafed than its sativa cousins.*

The Main Chemical Elements of Marijuana

Both the *sativa* and *indica* species of cannabis contain more than 480 identifiable chemical compounds. Dozens of these chemicals have psychoactive properties that account for the physical, emotional, and behavioral changes associated with marijuana use. But the concentrations of these cannabis compounds, known as cannabinoids, vary considerably within the *sativa* and *indica* strains and their many hybrids.

Of the many psychoactive cannabinoids found in marijuana, two common and powerful cannabinoids account for most of the narcotic effects of marijuana—THC and cannabidiol (CBD). The highest concentrations of THC and CBD are found in the flowering tops, or buds, of cannabis plants. Marijuana leaves also contain these cannabinoids in significant amounts, so they are harvested by growers as well. Cannabis seeds and stems, however, contain far smaller concentrations of psychoactive chemicals. As a result, marijuana growers filter these parts of the plant out of their final product.

THC is the main intoxicating chemical in *Cannabis sativa*, which usually only contains low amounts of CBD. Scientists say that THC is the compound most responsible for the enhanced senses and exhilarating high feeling often associated with marijuana consumption. The highest concentrations of THC are

A colored electron micrograph reveals brown crystals of tetrahydrocannabinol (THC) on the surface of processed marijuana. THC is the active ingredient in marijuana.

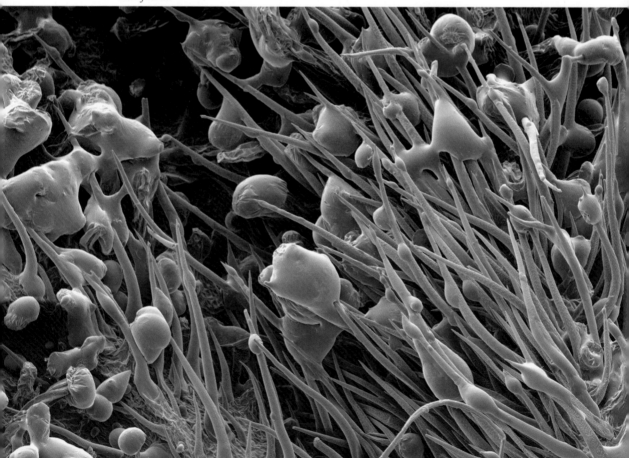

found in the buds of female cannabis plants that remain unfertilized from male, pollen-producing plants. These unfertilized tops or buds can be harvested to create a particularly strong type of marijuana known as sinsemilla, which has very high THC levels. Female plants that have been fertilized, on the other hand, focus on producing seeds rather than buds, which makes them much less valuable. That is why marijuana growers work hard to weed male plants out of their operations (although male plants may be kept for breeding purposes).

A More Important Issue than People Realize

"The people that bother me the most . . . [are progressives who] dismiss marijuana policy with kind of a little giggle and ask me why I would waste my time and political capital on it. The people who still think that it's not a serious issue. . . . It's not just an irritation for some people; this [criminalization of marijuana] is actually doing harm to our country. The War on Drugs has made us the number-one jailer nation on the planet—and all educated and concerned citizens should know that and want to do something about it."—Pete Holmes, a Seattle attorney who helped build support for the passage of a marijuana legalization referendum in the state of Washington in 2012

Quoted in David Bienenstock. "After Legalization, What's Next? Attorney Who Helped Free the Weed in Washington State Talks Strategy." AlterNet, December 13, 2012. www.alternet.org/drugs/after-legalization-whats-next-attorney-who-helped-free-weed -washington-state-talks-strategy?page=0%2C0.

THC is also present in *Cannabis indica*, but in more moderate amounts. The main cannabinoid in *Cannabis indica* is CBD. This psychoactive works as more of a sedative than THC does. It also tends to produce more body-centered effects (like dry mouth, sleepiness, and enhanced physical sensations) than do THC-heavy strains of marijuana. As with *Cannabis sativa* producers, growers of *Cannabis indica* boost the volume and potency of their crop by keeping their bud-generating female plants away from the pollen of male plants.

A third major cannabinoid, called cannabinol (CBN), is also present in many strains of marijuana. CBN is actually produced

Delivered from Pain by Marijuana

In 1911 Dorothy Gibbs contracted polio as an infant and lost most of the use of her legs. In the late 1990s the elderly woman's quality of life declined dramatically due to severe osteoarthritis. Her pain levels spiked, and her doctors were unable to find any prescription drugs that could relieve her misery. In 1997, though, Gibbs's caretaker convinced her to try marijuana. According to Gibbs, the drug gave her a new lease on life:

> The relief I experienced from medical marijuana was almost immediate. . . . I strongly feel that I should have the right to use anything that may relieve any or some of my pain, and my last days should not be spent suffering. . . . Although chronic pain related to my post-polio syndrome will always be a part of my life, medical marijuana has helped me manage this pain by providing fast and effective relief for my muscle spasms, acute pains, and arthritis.

Quoted in Americans for Safe Access. *Chronic Pain and Medical Cannabis*. Washington, DC: ASA, 2011, pp. 14–15.

as THC ages and breaks down upon exposure to air. This natural process is known as oxidization. "This is why cannabis that has been left unused will have increasing amounts of CBN and decreasing amounts of THC and thus lose potency,"[24] states Australia's National Cannabis Prevention and Information Centre.

Marijuana and the Human Body

The chemicals contained in marijuana can be taken into the human body in several different ways. The most familiar method is to smoke and inhale it, from either a pipe or a hand-rolled cigarette known as a joint. One particularly popular type of pipe used by both medicinal and recreational users of marijuana is called a bong. This is a large pipe that includes a tube filled with water, which cools off the smoke before it is inhaled. Whatever method is employed for inhaling marijuana smoke, the fumes enter the lungs. From there the cannabinoids pass into the bloodstream and are carried to the brain.

Vaporization is another method by which some people use marijuana without inhaling smoke. In this case cannabis is placed in a heating device that converts the plant's THC and other cannabinoids into a vapor that can be collected and inhaled. The resulting vapors contain none of the toxic by-products found in marijuana smoke, which means that respiratory risks sometimes associated with smoking marijuana are eliminated.

Some people prefer to consume cannabis by ingesting it. They drink tea made from shredded marijuana leaves; eat muffins, cookies, brownies, or candy-type products that feature cannabis ingredients; swallow cannabis-filled capsules; or use cooking oils made from cannabinoids. When marijuana is ingested rather than inhaled, THC and other psychoactives enter the bloodstream through the lining of the stomach. They then travel through the bloodstream to the brain.

The acute sensitivity of humans to marijuana is due to the fact that the human brain produces a naturally occurring neurotransmitter known as anandamide, which is very similar in structure to THC. The Hash, Marihuana & Hemp Museum in Amsterdam, Netherlands, explains:

> Receptors for anandamide are found throughout the human body—in the nervous system, gut, organs, and especially in the brain. The collective name for this network is the endocannabinoid system. Because of this system, the cannabinoids contained in cannabis are able to bind to the endocannabinoid receptors present in the human body. This action is the basis of all the psychoactive and most of the medical benefits of cannabis.[25]

Medical Applications for Cannabis

Different blends of medical marijuana are now commonly used in the treatment of many different diseases and conditions. Generally, medical marijuana is seen not as a cure for disease, but rather as a palliative—a drug that can help relieve or lessen the symptoms of a disease or disorder.

The closest thing to an exception to this rule of thumb can be found in cannabis treatments for glaucoma, an incurable medical condition that is the second leading cause of blindness in the United States. The onset of glaucoma is associated with a buildup of pressure inside the eye, a phenomenon called intraocular pressure (IOP). This pressure can take a heavy toll on the eye's optic nerve and cause total and permanent loss of vision within a few years. Some studies and personal testimonials from patients suffering from IOP indicate that medical marijuana might be useful in reducing this pressure and thus stopping the advance of glaucoma. Other scientists and health-care professionals specializing in glaucoma treatment, however, assert that a number of glaucoma drugs on the market provide levels of IOP relief that are similar to cannabis but without the side effects of pot.

Therapeutic Effects of Cannabis

Therapeutic effect	Therapeutic use
Bronchodilation	Bronchial asthma
Antiemetic effect	Prevention of nausea/vomiting caused by anticancer drugs
Appetite stimulation	Palliative care for anorexia caused by opioids, antiviral drugs, AIDS–related illnesses or terminal cancer
Analgesia	Cancer pain, post–operative pain, phantom limb pain
Decreased spasticity/ataxia/muscle weakness	Multiple sclerosis, cerebral palsy, spinal cord injuries
Decreased intraocular pressure	Glaucoma

Taken from: *Journal of Psychoactive Drugs,* Apr–June, 2011.

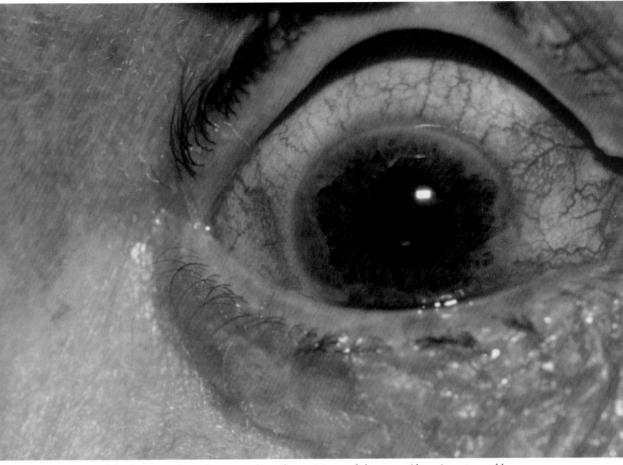

Marijuana has been shown to relieve the symptoms of glaucoma (shown), an incurable medical condition that is the second-leading cause of blindness in the United States.

Marijuana has also become a common sight in the medicine cabinets of patients suffering from HIV/AIDS and many different forms of cancer. Cannabis consumption is known to stimulate appetite, a phenomenon popularly known as "getting the munchies." This can benefit people with HIV/AIDS and cancer who often suffer loss of appetite and associated declines in body weight, muscle mass, and energy. These declines in appetite and health typically stem not only from the disease itself, but from other medical treatments (like chemotherapy for cancer) that cause nausea and vomiting. Researchers have shown that medical cannabis can suppress these symptoms and treatment side effects and help patients maintain healthier weight while battling illness.

Medical marijuana has also emerged as a popular pain-management tool. Many patients report—and scientific studies seem to confirm—that medical cannabis can reduce levels of acute or chronic pain associated with a wide range of illnesses and disorders. According to Americans for Safe Access (ASA), a pro-legalization group, nearly three hundred studies conducted from 1975 to early 2011 indicated that cannabinoids and cannabis were helpful to patients experiencing chronic pain. "A number of areas in the brain that have an established role in sensing and processing pain respond to the analgesic effect of cannabis," states the ASA. "Cannabinoids have been used suc-

A Parkinson's patient consults with his doctor. Medical researchers have called for new studies to assess the usefulness of cannabinoids in extending life expectancy and improving quality of life for people with glaucoma, ALS, MS, and Parkinson's disease.

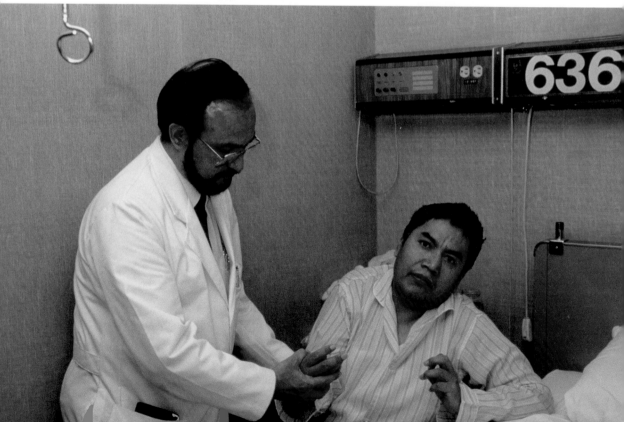

cessfully to treat cancer pain, which is often resistant to treatment with opiates."[26]

Some people who are grappling with muscle-control disorders have also turned to medical marijuana. These patients range from people with mild and irregular muscle spasms to those who suffer from serious conditions like multiple sclerosis (MS), which afflicts about three hundred thousand Americans; amyotrophic lateral sclerosis (ALS), or Lou Gehrig's disease, which impacts about thirty thousand Americans; and Parkinson's disease, a disorder affecting about half a million Americans. Symptoms of all three of these neuromuscular diseases include severe muscle stiffness and involuntary muscle contractions, spasms, and tremors. Some patients with these diseases say that medical cannabis has helped them stave off the worst effects. As a result, medical researchers have called for new studies to assess the usefulness of cannabinoids in extending life expectancy and improving quality of life for people with ALS, MS, and Parkinson's disease.

Smoking Illegal Drugs Is Not the Answer

"We have a responsibility as a civilized society to ensure that the medicine Americans receive from their doctors is effective, safe and free from the pro-drug politics that are being promoted in America under the guise of medicine. Smoking illegal drugs may make some people 'feel better.' However, civilized societies and modern day medical practices differentiate between inebriation and the safe, supervised delivery of proven medicine by legitimate doctors."—Office of National Drug Control Policy director John Walters

Quoted in Tanya Albert. "Supreme Court Quashes Use of Medical Marijuana." *American Medical News*, June 27, 2005. www.amednews.com/article/20050627/government/306279979/4/.

Scientists are also studying medical marijuana's potential for relieving various types of arthritis and inflammatory joint conditions. These disorders can cause swollen joints that are not only painful but can also reduce mobility. Some patients dealing with chronic conditions like rheumatoid arthritis have already turned

The Issue of Medical Marijuana Diversion

In 2012 researchers at the University of Colorado released a study indicating that medical marijuana diversion—people using medical marijuana that is actually prescribed to someone else—may be a significant problem in states that have legalized pot for medical purposes. The scientists found that 74 percent of 164 adolescents in a state substance-abuse program admitted they got high using someone else's legally obtained medical cannabis. These teens also reported using diverted pot to get high on multiple occasions—the median usage among respondents who acknowledged consuming diverted marijuana was fifty times.

Critics of medical marijuana have cited this study as evidence that medical cannabis programs are being cynically exploited by huge numbers of recreational pot smokers. Other observers, however, caution not to read too much into the study. They note that since the teens in the study are already in substance-abuse programs, they are much more likely to have a history with drugs—including diverted drugs—than is the general population.

to medical cannabis for relief. Observers note that this willingness to explore medical marijuana to relieve joint pain can be partially attributed to the fact that some "pharmaceutical drugs prescribed to arthritis patients to produce the same results have many unpleasant and sometimes dangerous side-effects including ulcers, severe weight loss, and breathing problems."[27]

Another area of marijuana research concerns the plant's possible therapeutic value in treating Alzheimer's disease (which afflicts about 4.5 million Americans) and other forms of dementia. Recreational marijuana use is notorious for causing some level of short-term memory loss. Yet a number of recent academic studies indicate that THC, pot's leading cannabinoid, may actually promote the growth of new brain cells in elderly people and slow the progression of memory loss to a degree that currently approved prescription drugs cannot match.

Finally, advocates of medical marijuana have hailed the plant's capacity to address insomnia, which bothers millions of

Americans to one degree or another. This benefit is of particular interest to patients with chronic pain or other health issues that make it more difficult for them to get a good night's sleep.

Obtaining a Recommendation for Medical Marijuana

In states that have approved marijuana for medical purposes, the laws governing the operations of commercial growers and dispensaries differ in various respects. Similarly, Americans who wish to use medical marijuana for treatment of any disorder or disease must follow certain state-specific procedures to obtain the drug legally. Broadly speaking, however, the requirements for selling and obtaining medical cannabis are fairly similar.

The first hurdle for prospective purchasers of medical marijuana is to obtain a doctor's approval for use. Even in states that have legalized marijuana for medical purposes, though, physicians are barred by law from actually prescribing the drug. By

A Colorado medical marijuana dispensary owner displays his license to sell medical marijuana and a sample of his wares. In states that have approved marijuana for medical purposes, the laws governing the operations of commercial growers and dispensaries differ in various details.

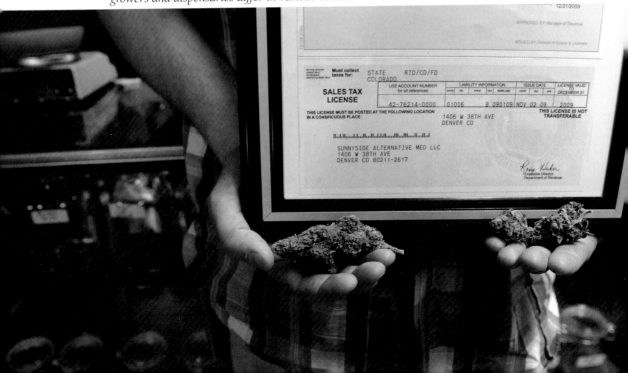

2014 medical marijuana laws had been crafted so that only state or municipal authorities can actually authorize the use of marijuana by a resident—and even then only for the treatment of certain illnesses or conditions. State medical marijuana programs do, however, require a state-approved and certified doctor's *recommendation* for medical marijuana treatment before they will grant permission to a patient.

Not all physicians are comfortable making such a recommendation. Some express concerns about the fact that the marijuana trade is still illegal according to federal law. Others refuse to participate in state or municipal marijuana programs because of personal or professional objections to medical marijuana. Generally, however, it is not difficult to find a doctor who participates in a state program. Some doctors openly advertise on the Internet or in local yellow pages their willingness to make recommendations. Medical marijuana dispensaries also maintain lists of doctors who will issue medical cannabis treatment recommendations. "It's basically a doctor's opinion [the state] is relying on," writes Matt Labash. "You may have to do one or two visits. But it wouldn't take you long"[28] to get a recommendation.

In several states that have passed medical marijuana laws, entire physicians' groups have been established for the express purpose of issuing recommendations. In Michigan, for example, the Cannabis Physicians Group has locations in more than a half-dozen cities across the southern half of the state. The group charges a $150 fee for its service, and the state charges another $100 to process the patient's application. Michigan's processing fee is in line with the fees that most other states charge to prospective medical marijuana users.

Patients who are approved for medical cannabis receive a medical marijuana card from the state. Patients are required to present this identification card at state-authorized dispensaries before they can purchase medical marijuana. In most states with medical marijuana programs, these cards are only valid for twelve months but can be renewed.

CHAPTER 3

THE BENEFITS OF LEGALIZING MEDICAL MARIJUANA

Advocates of medical marijuana bring many arguments to bear in the ongoing debate over legalization. First and foremost, they claim that legalizing medical cannabis would improve the health and quality of life of tens of thousands of patients suffering from a wide range of diseases and medical conditions. They also claim, however, that the legalization of medical marijuana would bring a number of important social benefits.

Calls for Increased Research

The therapeutic benefits of medical marijuana have been hailed by numerous organizations of physicians, nurses, and other caregivers. The American Public Health Association, the American Nurses Association, and the California Pharmacists Association have all passed formal resolutions in support of medical marijuana. Other organizations that have held off on issuing formal endorsements of medical pot, such as the American Medical Association (AMA), have nonetheless urged the federal government to review its designation of marijuana as a Schedule I controlled substance. The AMA says that the government's insistence on keeping marijuana a Schedule I drug has made it much more difficult to conduct research into the plant's therapeutic properties.

The American College of Physicians has leveled the same complaint about the roadblocks that federal authorities have erected against marijuana research. In an official 2008 position paper, the group insisted that "additional research is needed to clarify marijuana's therapeutic properties and determine standard and optimal doses and routes of delivery."[29]

Advocates of medical cannabis also emphasize that loosening research restrictions on the plant would not necessarily result in laws legalizing pot for recreational purposes. As Mark Eddy of the Congressional Research Service explains, rescheduling marijuana "would put it on a par with cocaine, methamphetamine, morphine, and methadone, all of which are Schedule II substances that are not close to becoming legal for recreational use."[30]

THC is extracted from marijuana in a research facility. Advocates of medical cannabis emphasize that loosening research restrictions on the plant would not necessarily result in laws legalizing pot for recreational purposes.

Health Professionals Tout Benefits

Many physicians who support medical marijuana believe that expanded research would simply confirm what they already know: that the plant is clearly effective in reducing chronic pain, muscle spasms, nausea, and anxiety, and that it has a proven capacity to lift the spirits and morale of patients. "Thousands of patients with cancer, AIDS, and other diseases report they have obtained striking relief from . . . devastating symptoms by smoking marijuana," stated the editor in chief of the influential *New England Journal of Medicine* in 1997. "I believe that a federal policy that prohibits physicians from alleviating suffering by prescribing marijuana for seriously ill patients is misguided, heavy-handed, and inhumane."[31]

Respected researchers have joined physicians, nurses, and patient advocates in championing marijuana's medical benefits. Gregory Carter, a physician, professor, and codirector of the Muscular Dystrophy Association/Amyotrophic Lateral Sclerosis Center, testified in 2007:

> I have spent my entire career in search of more effective treatments for this awful disease [amyotrophic lateral sclerosis, or Lou Gehrig's disease]. We have now found that the . . . active ingredients in medical marijuana work remarkably well in controlling the clinical symptoms of ALS. Even more exciting is that we are now discovering that the cannabinoids actually protect nerve cells and may prolong the life of patients with ALS.[32]

Harvey L. Rose, a teacher at the University of California–Davis School of Medicine, offered a similar assessment:

> Both my research and my many years as a clinician have convinced me that marijuana can serve at least two important roles in safe and effective pain management. Ample anecdotal evidence and clinical observations, as well as significant research findings, strongly indicate that marijuana, for whatever reason, is often effective in

An ALS patient purchases medical marijuana at a Colorado dispensary. Studies have shown that the active ingredients in medical marijuana help control some of the clinical symptoms of ALS.

relieving pain. This is true across a range of patient populations, including the elderly, the terminally ill seeking comfort in their final days, young adults stricken with life-threatening conditions, and cancer patients unable to tolerate the devastating effects of potentially life-saving therapies.[33]

The Best Option for Some Patients

Opponents say that legalizing medical marijuana is not necessary, because pharmaceutical drugs approved by the U.S. Food and Drug Administration (FDA) can address the needs and relieve the ailments of patients. Pro-marijuana forces disagree with this sentiment. "Smoking [marijuana] can actually be a preferred drug delivery system for patients whose nausea prevents them from taking anything orally," notes one report on medical cannabis. "Other patients *prefer* inhaling because the drug is absorbed much more quickly through the lungs, so that the beneficial effects of the drug are felt almost at once."[34]

"THE VAPOR OF REEFER MADNESS"

"What's left for those still grasping at the vapor of reefer madness? Only the illogical concept that admitting that marijuana prohibition has been a terrible, foolish mistake, which should be reversed so that it can help ease the suffering of the critically ill, is somehow sending the wrong message to our children."—Journalist Greg Campbell

Greg Campbell. *Pot, Inc.: Inside Medical Marijuana, America's Most Outlaw Industry*. New York: Sterling, 2012, p. 185.

Advocates of medical cannabis also reject claims that synthetic drugs that use THC, the best-known cannabinoid in marijuana, are equivalent to marijuana. Supporters of medical marijuana point out that prescriptions for Marinol and other synthetic pharmaceuticals developed by big drug companies carry a much higher price tag than marijuana plants, which can be raised quickly and inexpensively. Marijuana advocates also claim that for many patients Marinol simply does not work as well as natural marijuana. Cannabis plants contain dozens of known active cannabinoids in addition to THC, which is the only cannabinoid contained in Marinol. Advocates of medical marijuana believe that some of these other cannabinoids may also play an important role in alleviating pain and providing therapeutic benefits.

Medical marijuana supporters contend that expanded research will eventually help scientists better understand how these cannabinoids work together. In the meantime, though, these supporters insist that American lawmakers and health-care professionals should not ignore the fact that, as one Congressional Research Service report put it, "many medical marijuana users report trying cannabis only reluctantly and as a last resort after exhausting all other treatment modalities. A distinct subpopulation of patients now relies on whole cannabis for a degree of relief that FDA-approved synthetic drugs do not provide."[35]

Many advocates of medical cannabis thus press the idea that marijuana should be used instead of—or at least in combination with—other prescription drugs. They highlight the experiences of patients who say that marijuana provided relief from pain and nausea caused by illnesses like AIDS and multiple sclerosis. In addition, its properties have helped alleviate the negative side effects of harsh drugs or chemotherapy treatments that are used to fight cancer and other diseases. "Within the medical-marijuana community, it [is] well known that cannabis helped patients cut down or eliminate heavy doses of narcotic painkillers,"[36] writes journalist Martin A. Lee.

Numerous studies have shown that the pain-relieving properties of THC and other cannabinoids in marijuana can reduce patients' reliance on aspirin, ibuprofen, and other nonsteroidal anti-inflammatory drugs (NSAIDs) that carry their own health risks, such as kidney failure and intestinal bleeding. "Acetaminophen, [an] NSAID widely used as an over-the-counter pain reliever for children, has been linked to asthma and other ailments," says Lee. "NSAIDs reportedly contribute to more than 100,000 hospitalizations and 16,500 deaths annually in the United States."[37]

Safe to Use

Proponents of medical marijuana charge that opponents routinely exaggerate the health hazards of marijuana use. Scholars Wendy Chapkis and Richard J. Webb write that despite investing huge amounts of money into research "seeking to establish the dangers of the drug," the federal government has found little evidence that it is harmful. They add, "The National Institute

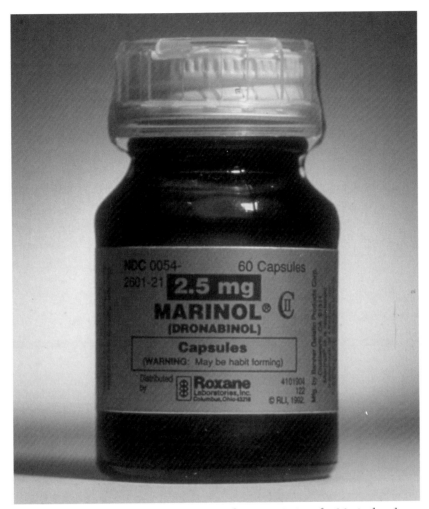

Supporters of medical marijuana point out that prescriptions for Marinol and other synthetic cannabinoid pharmaceuticals developed by big drug companies carry a much higher price tag than marijuana, which can be raised quickly and inexpensively.

of Medicine (IOM) and the World Health Organization (WHO) both have concluded that the effects of marijuana are relatively benign."[38]

Researchers acknowledge that marijuana smoke contains some of the same cancer-causing compounds as tobacco smoke. With this in mind, some legalization advocates have pointed to vaporizers or marijuana-laced baked goods as options for people

"Marijuana Never Fails to Lift My Mood"

Suzanne Pfeil of California suffers from post-polio syndrome, a chronic condition with symptoms that include severe nerve and muscle pain. According to Pfeil, marijuana is the best medicine she has found for relieving that pain. She explains:

> When I get a pain flair, I smoke it and it helps to relieve the pain and relieve the spasms but it also means I don't get as depressed. . . . Marijuana never fails to lift my mood. I smoke and think,

"OK, I'm just going to have to go with the pain today. It's beautiful outside and I'm going to go tool around the garden in my chair." . . . The other drugs I'm prescribed have such major side effects, but if I smoke a joint, the biggest side effect is a mental lift. And that's a side effect I can live with.

Quoted in Wendy Chapkis and Richard J. Webb. *Dying to Get High: Marijuana as Medicine.* New York: New York University Press, 2008, p. 121.

who worry that regular pot smoking could increase their vulnerability to emphysema, cancer, or chronic lung disease. Medical cannabis supporters emphasize, though, that scientific studies have not established any clear link between smoking marijuana and diseases like lung cancer, even among heavy pot smokers. A major study released in 2006 by the National Institute on Drug Abuse (NIDA) even suggested that regular marijuana use might inhibit cancer. Researchers at the NIDA theorized that regular intake of the cannabinoid THC might kill aging cells that otherwise run a higher risk of turning cancerous.

Medical marijuana supporters also like to remind people that some products with well-known health risks—especially tobacco and alcohol—are commercially available and heavily consumed in the United States for recreational purposes. Attorney Anthony Cotton writes:

> Marijuana does not create dependency, and people do not go through withdrawal when they stop using [pot]. . . . The same cannot be said for countless other sub-

stances that are legal and flow freely in the community.
. . . Do these laws make sense? Ask any prosecutors
when they last saw a domestic violence case in which a
husband got stoned and decided to attack his wife. Ask
those same prosecutors how often they see domestic violence cases involving alcohol.[39]

Many potent pharmaceutical drugs are also commonly prescribed by doctors to address pain or for other therapeutic reasons, even though these drugs are sometimes abused or even

*Some legalization advocates have pointed to vaporizers (pictured) or marijuana-
laced baked goods as options for people who worry that regular pot smoking could
increase their vulnerability to emphysema, lung cancer, or chronic lung disease.*

used to commit suicide. Meanwhile, journalist Greg Campbell points out:

> Scientists have not been able to determine a lethal dose for marijuana. No deaths due to overdose have ever been substantiated in all of recorded human history. You can suffer a fatal overdose of water or potatoes, but scientists have never been able to kill test animals with marijuana (except by asphyxiating them with pot smoke). It's estimated that to kill yourself with pot, you would need to smoke 1,500 pounds of marijuana in 15 minutes, which is, of course, physically impossible. And even that's a guess.[40]

The Benefits of Mood Enhancement

Another aspect of medical cannabis use that advocates defend is the high that patients experience from smoking or ingesting the plant. Supporters acknowledge that recreational pot users seek to get high simply because they like the feeling, but supporters believe that some people grappling with serious health issues benefit enormously when they enter this state of altered consciousness. As one AIDS patient explains:

> Marijuana lifts me up past whatever symptoms I have at the moment and creates this sense of wellness and well-being that allows me to just function very much the way I could before I was HIV positive. I really feel like the worst symptom of HIV is how drained it makes you feel. The feeling of well-being that we all take for granted when we are healthy, that mental state disappears when we feel sick. So when I'm stoned, I'm able to just rise above it and press on. . . . When you are really sick it affects your desire to live. . . . So if you can take some substance to make you feel well, even for a brief moment in time to remind you what that's like, it's invaluable.[41]

The pro-legalization camp also embraces the old saying that "laughter is the best medicine." Lee explains, "Marijuana makes people laugh, and laughter is therapeutic. Laughter is excellent medicine for reducing stress, boosting the immune system, and increasing oxygenation and blood flow. . . . A good belly laugh can exercise the heart more efficiently than a physical workout. Laughter can even help type-2 diabetics process sugar better."[42]

These considerations have led some physicians and medical researchers who support medical marijuana to defend the drug's high as a contributing factor in its overall usefulness as a health-care tool. "There are many health professionals who perceive that a mild psychoactive effect from the drug is somehow wrong," says William Notcutt, a researcher who helped develop a synthetic marijuana substitute called Sativex. "This only seems to be of concern to those who do not treat patients in pain or distress. . . . Elevating the mood of a patient whose life is miserable because of chronic, untreatable pain would seem to be a worthwhile goal."[43]

Dr. William Notcutt, a researcher who helped develop the synthetic marijuana substitute Sativex (shown), claims that concerns about marijuana patients' getting high from their therapeutic use of the plant are not warranted.

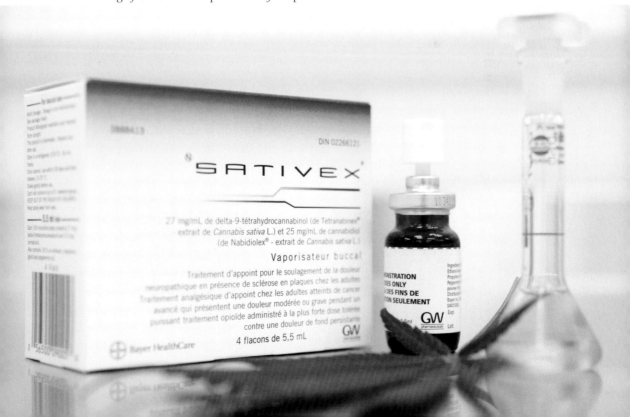

Overblown Gateway Drug Fears

Supporters of medical marijuana also reject the notion that state-approved pot will serve as a "gateway drug" to other illegal drugs that are more universally regarded as destructive and addictive, like heroin and cocaine. Pro-marijuana groups contend that research studies have failed to establish a linkage between marijuana use and higher levels of cocaine or heroin use. On the contrary, the prestigious Institute of Medicine flatly states that "most drug users do not begin their drug use with marijuana—they begin with alcohol and nicotine, usually when they are too young to do so legally."[44]

Claims that marijuana is a gateway drug have also received little support from government studies. Scholar James Austin points out that according to a 2003 study by the U.S. Department of Health and Human Services,

> over 25 million [Americans] consume marijuana each year with nearly 15 million using the drug in the past month. By way of comparison, very small percentages of Americans (under 4 percent in total) have used cocaine, crack, heroin or other inhalants in the past 30 days. So somewhere along the line, the vast majority of the marijuana drug users do not graduate to the more dangerous drugs.[45]

Medical marijuana advocates also highlight studies that have examined whether teen pot smoking jumped in states that have passed medical marijuana laws. Of the thirteen states with effective medical marijuana laws with before-and-after data on teen marijuana use, only the two with the most recently enacted laws (Michigan and New Mexico) indicated possible increases, according to a 2011 academic analysis sponsored by the pro-legalization Marijuana Policy Project (MPP). Most states, however, reported overall decreases in teen pot use, "strongly suggesting that enactment of state medical marijuana laws does not increase teen marijuana use,"[46] according to the MPP.

Social and Economic Benefits

Many pro-pot groups see legalization of medical marijuana as the first step in a wider effort to decriminalize marijuana for recreational use. "Medical marijuana is an important issue in and of itself," writes Campbell, "but it is being used as a vehicle for broader acceptance with the hope that it will eventually be legalized in the same way as alcohol and tobacco."[47] At that point, proponents say, the social and economic benefits of legalization will quickly become evident. These benefits would include smarter allocation of law enforcement resources, improved career and economic opportunities for young minorities, and reductions in crime.

MARIJUANA MORE DANGEROUS THAN COCAINE?

"For more than thirty years, the federal government has been dispensing government-grown reefer to a handful of medical-necessity patients, while the DEA, FDA, and NIDA pretend that marijuana lacks therapeutic value. Riddled with contradictions, federal policy ranks Schedule I cannabis as more dangerous than Schedule II crack cocaine. It makes no sense. Why is it legal for a corporation to sell THC, but it's not legal to get the very same compound by growing a plant in your own garden? What's up with that?"—Journalist Martin A. Lee

Martin A. Lee. *Smoke Signals: A Social History of Marijuana—Medical, Recreational, and Scientific.* New York: Scribner, 2012, p. 403.

Supporters of pot legalization point out that marijuana sales have long been a lucrative source of income for Mexican drug cartels and American gangs alike. By some estimates, Mexican drug lords make as much as 70 percent of their income from marijuana sales in the United States. Meanwhile, gang members constitute an important sales force for the cartels. The money that gangs make from selling marijuana in America's cities and suburbs helps keep them afloat and gives them the ability to finance other criminal activities. Advocates of marijuana legalization argue that if marijuana were legalized and regulated, the drug cartels and gangs would lose much of their power and influence.

Supporters of legalization also say that legalizing marijuana would free the criminal justice system to allocate its resources to

The Tragic Story of Jonathan Magbie

Jonathan Magbie was four years old when he was paralyzed from the neck down in a car collision with a drunk driver. From that point forward, he required virtually round-the-clock medical care, as well as a device called a ventilator in order to breathe while sleeping. As he grew older, Magbie discovered that marijuana eased the discomfort of his condition. In 2004, however, the twenty-seven-year-old Magbie was arrested for marijuana possession. Washington, D.C., judge Judith E. Retchin sentenced him to ten days in jail, even though it was his first offense and she knew that the city's jails were not equipped to handle his ventilator. Once Magbie entered the jail, his physical condition quickly deteriorated. He was finally transferred to a hospital after four days, but by that point his life was slipping away. He died on September 24, 2004, of heart failure.

Magbie's grieving family filed a lawsuit against the city of Washington, D.C., and the hospital. The lawsuit was eventually settled out of court for an undisclosed financial payment, as well as guarantees that correctional officials would implement policies to better protect prisoners with medical problems and physical disabilities. Retchin remained on the bench until her retirement in 2010.

Jonathan Magbie's family mourns him at his funeral.

more serious crimes. In the process, they say, it would give a big economic and spiritual lift to black and Hispanic communities that account for a disproportionate share of marijuana arrests and prosecutions. According to the MPP, federal statistics from 2010 indicated that 11 percent of marijuana users were black and 74 percent white. Yet blacks accounted for 32 percent of marijuana arrests and 44 percent of convictions nationally that year.

Similar findings have led some black civil rights activists to support calls for marijuana legalization. "We have empirical proof that the application of the marijuana laws has been unfairly applied to our young people of color," said Alice Huffman, president of the California branch of the National Association for the Advancement of Colored People, in 2010. "Justice is the quality of being just and fair and these laws have been neither just nor fair."[48]

Finally, proponents of marijuana legalization say that legalizing marijuana would spark new industries that would generate new jobs and tax revenue for communities across the country. They point out that states that have passed medical marijuana laws have already reaped some of these tax benefits. In Oregon, for example, the state has used higher enrollment fees from its medical marijuana program to fund a wide assortment of other health programs that benefit residents across the state. In Michigan the state pulled in more than $10 million in tax revenue from medical marijuana dispensaries in 2012 alone.

THE DRAWBACKS OF LEGALIZING MEDICAL MARIJUANA

Critics of medical marijuana have raised numerous objections to legalization of the drug. They protest that cannabis has not been adequately tested, that it is impossible to control the dosage, and that it will make workplaces and roadways more dangerous. Opponents also charge that increased acceptance of medical marijuana will damage law enforcement efforts to keep young people from smoking pot for recreational purposes and that it will lead young people to abuse harder drugs. Many organizations opposed to medical marijuana believe, in fact, that the legalization push is no more than a deceitful effort to end prohibitions on the sale, possession, and use of the plant for any purpose, including getting high for enjoyment.

Heightened Health Risks from Smoking Marijuana

The Drug Free America Foundation calls proposals to medicate patients with marijuana "a step backward to the times of potions and herbal remedies."[49] This position reflects the fact that marijuana has not yet been subject to the same rigorous scientific testing as other drugs that have been approved by the FDA, the federal agency responsible for overseeing pharmaceutical drugs in the United States. The American Society of Addiction Medicine (ASAM) states:

> The practice of medicine is increasingly evidence-based, yet some physicians are willing to consider "recommending"

cannabis to their patients, despite the fact that they lack even the most rudimentary information about the material (composition, quality, and dose). . . . Pharmaceutical companies are responsible for the harms caused by contaminated or otherwise dangerous products and tobacco companies can be held accountable for harms caused by cigarettes, yet, dispensaries distribute cannabis products about which very little are known, including their source.[50]

Some of the limited studies that have been undertaken indicate possible health benefits associated with marijuana intake. These positive results mostly concern the drug's capacity to relieve pain, nausea, and other problems that are either

The therapeutic properties of marijuana are studied in a lab. Many oppose medical marijuana because it has not yet been subjected to the same rigorous testing as other drugs approved by the Food and Drug Administration.

symptoms of disease or side effects of FDA-approved drugs. Opponents of legalization, however, counter by highlighting studies that cast doubt on marijuana's medical value. These studies either minimize the extent of marijuana's benefits or indicate that medical use of the plant poses potentially serious health dangers.

Many of the alleged health risks associated with marijuana use center on the fact that it is usually taken into the body by inhaling smoke from burning pot. Marijuana contains more than four hundred chemicals, including most of the harmful substances found in tobacco smoke. Scientists also say that smoking one marijuana cigarette deposits about four times more tar into the lungs than a cigarette of tobacco. "Can you think of any other untested, home-made, mind-altering medicine that you self-dose, and that uses a burning carcinogen as a delivery vehicle?"[51] asks General Barry McCaffrey, who served as leader of the Office of National Drug Control Policy, the federal government's leading antidrug agency, from 1996 to 2000.

Critics assert that people who regularly smoke marijuana are at higher risk of contracting the same respiratory problems that afflict many cigarette smokers, including chronic cough and bronchitis. "If any components of marijuana are ever shown to be beneficial to treat any illness then those components can and should be delivered by nontoxic routes of administration in controlled doses just [like] all other medicines are in the U.S.," declares the ASAM. "ASAM rejects smoking as a means of drug delivery since it is not safe."[52]

Although studies of linkages between marijuana use and lung cancer have been sparse—and some of the ones that have been undertaken have failed to establish such a link—marijuana critics express confidence that scientists will eventually confirm a relationship. They point, for example, to several European medical researchers whose recent findings suggest that smoking cannabis could increase the risk of developing lung cancer. At the very least, critics of medical marijuana say that cannabis consumption should be halted until more is known about its impact on human respiratory systems.

Other Safety Concerns

Opponents of medical marijuana have also alleged other health dangers associated with cannabis. They charge that it can increase the risk of heart attacks and weaken immune systems in ways that leave patients more vulnerable to lung infections and other ailments. In addition, critics point out that pot is notorious for interfering with memory, concentration, body coordination, and decision-making ability—a fact that even marijuana supporters acknowledge. It can also trigger unpleasant feelings of paranoia, panic, or anxiety.

Marijuana use has been known to affect the eyes, the central nervous, circulatory, reproductive, and respiratory systems, as well as the stomach and intestines.

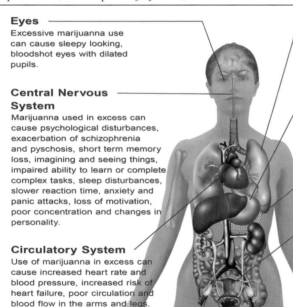

Eyes
Excessive marijuanna use can cause sleepy looking, bloodshot eyes with dilated pupils.

Central Nervous System
Marijuanna used in excess can cause psychological disturbances, exacerbation of schizophrenia and pyschosis, short term memory loss, imagining and seeing things, impaired ability to learn or complete complex tasks, sleep disturbances, slower reaction time, anxiety and panic attacks, loss of motivation, poor concentration and changes in personality.

Circulatory System
Use of marijuanna in excess can cause increased heart rate and blood pressure, increased risk of heart failure, poor circulation and blood flow in the arms and legs.

Respiratory System
Use of marijuanna increases the risk of chest infections, lung, mouth and throat cancer as well as chronic bronchitis and emphysema.

Stomach and Intestines
Marijuanna used in excess can cause the stomach and intestinal lining to become tender, bleed, develop ulcers and may lead to cancer.

Pancreas
Excess marijuanna use can cause increased risk of cancer.

Reproductive System
Excessive marijuanna use can decrease sperm count in men, lower sex drive, cause egg damage and irregular menstrual cycles, impair fertility, alter hormone levels in women and cause lowered birth weight, fetal abnormalities, poor growth, development and irritability.

The Effects of Marijuana on the Body

Addicted to Marijuana?

As the fierce debate over medical mari-juana continues, one consideration that is often overlooked is whether marijuana is addictive. For many years pro-legalization forces claimed to have the advantage on this issue. They quoted physicians and researchers who agreed that people who stop smoking marijuana do not suffer the clearly defined withdrawal symptoms that afflicted individuals who stop us-ing heroin, alcohol, tobacco, and other physically addictive substances suffer.

More recently, however, researchers have estimated that for perhaps 10 percent of users, marijuana can be *psychologically* addictive to the point that it impairs per-sonal relationships and workplace per-formance. This figure is still much lower than the addiction percentages for people who become dependent on alcohol, to-bacco, cocaine, and heroin, but it has giv-en antilegalization organizations another weapon to use in the debate over medical marijuana.

Mental health, in fact, is cited by some legalization critics as potentially an even more serious issue than cancer when it comes to medical and recreational marijuana use. "Marijuana has been linked clinically to the onset of depression, anxiety, and schizo-phrenia," writes journalist Andrew Ferguson. "The link is espe-cially strong in younger users and stronger still in young men with a predisposition to mental illness."[53]

Many of the illnesses, symptoms, and drug side effects that medical marijuana is used to address are also treatable with legal drugs that have been approved by the FDA. Opponents of legaliza-tion insist that in most cases, these FDA-approved pharmaceuti-cals are just as effective—or even more effective—than marijuana. Moreover, drugs that are approved by the FDA are dispensed in carefully calculated and measurable dosages to ensure safety and ef-fectiveness. In other words, one pill, capsule, teaspoon, or injection of FDA-approved medicine has the same amount of medicine as the next. By contrast, no such controls exist for marijuana dosages, since the chemical composition of each cannabis plant is different.

Opening the Doors to Increased Drug Abuse

Another major source of concern regarding medical marijuana legalization is that users of pot will "graduate" from pot to harder illegal drugs like heroin. Opponents of medical cannabis who raise this argument frequently point to the official position of the DEA. The agency has consistently maintained that marijuana is a gateway drug to cocaine, heroin, and other illicit and highly addictive drugs that damage or take thousands of lives every year. The DEA declared in 2011:

> Marijuana is a frequent precursor to the use of more dangerous drugs and signals a significantly enhanced likelihood of drug problems in adult life. . . . The *Journal of the American Medical Association* reported, based on a study of 300 sets of twins, "that marijuana-using twins were four times more likely than their siblings to use cocaine and crack cocaine, and five times more likely to use hallucinogens such as LSD." Long-term studies on patterns of drug usage among young people show that very few of them use other drugs without first starting with marijuana.[54]

Opponents of medical marijuana have also warned that in states that have approved medical prescriptions for cannabis, much of the pot that is supposedly being grown for medicinal purposes is really boosting the illegal drug trade in recreational marijuana. They claim that some marijuana dispensaries are little more than fronts for illegal narcotics sales. "State medical marijuana laws are routinely abused to facilitate traditional illegal trafficking,"[55] according to the Justice Department.

Police and other law enforcement organizations have complained that legalizing medical marijuana has made it extremely difficult for them to derail criminal marijuana growing and distribution operations. As the DEA states, "Local and state law enforcement counterparts cannot distinguish between illegal marijuana grows and grows that qualify as medical exemptions. Many self-designated medical marijuana growers are, in fact, growing marijuana for illegal, 'recreational' use."[56] Officers have also complained about the time-consuming aspects of determining whether people busted for marijuana growing or possession have the necessary legal approval to keep cannabis in their homes or cars.

Antilegalization organizations cite all of these factors in rejecting claims that legal but carefully regulated marijuana sales could provide an economic lift to communities and states. Opponents insist that tax revenues and jobs from a legally sanctioned marijuana industry would fail to match the financial costs of legalized pot. "Later on, we're going to pay triple or more in costs of new addictions than any new taxes are going to cover,"[57] explains a spokesperson for the Coalition for a Drug Free California.

Critics of medical marijuana say it is a gateway drug that can lead to addiction to harder drugs such as heroin (shown) and cocaine.

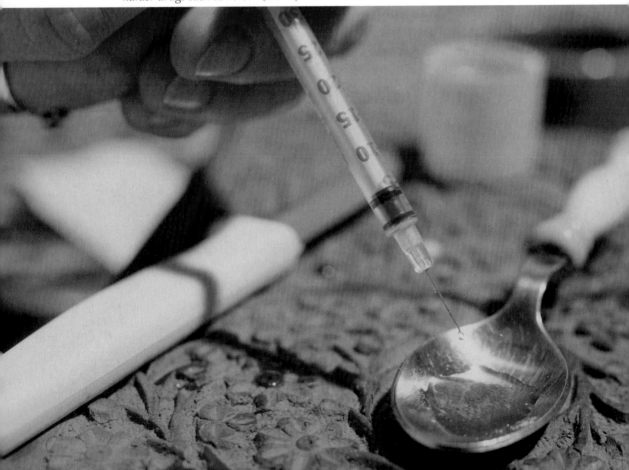

Rampant Misuse of Medical Marijuana

Opponents believe that many of the activists pushing for legalization of medical marijuana are just using the alleged health benefits of pot to advance their true goal—to legalize *all* marijuana use. The idea is that once medical marijuana becomes widely accepted in the United States and laws forbidding medical use of the plant have been eradicated, it will be much easier to tear down remaining laws that outlaw recreational use of pot. Critics have expressed great anger about this deceitful strategy, which they believe treats people with genuine health-care problems as pawns in the wider legalization crusade.

A Former Cannabis Advocate Changes His Mind

"I used to have fairly liberal views on cannabis . . . [but] I have become increasingly concerned in recent years that the drug is much more dangerous than we thought, and certainly nowhere as safe as most teenagers still think. . . . Most people consider cannabis to be much safer than tobacco but, drag for drag, it is actually more harmful. Cannabis smoke is far more acrid than tobacco and causes more damage to the lining of the airways. . . . And, like tobacco, it is packed with carcinogens."—Physician Mark Porter

Mark Porter. "Cannabis and the Risks: Facts You Need to Know." *Times* (London), February 14, 2009. www.thetimes.co.uk/tto/health/article1964344.ece.

Community leaders, lawmakers, and organizations lined up against medical marijuana believe that people in states that have approved medical marijuana are already manipulating the laws to obtain cannabis for recreational use. Writer Brett McCracken says:

Walk down the Venice or Santa Monica boardwalk in L.A. and you will be bombarded with leaflets for the dozens of medical marijuana dispensaries in town. Affable hippies even call out, "Get your medical marijuana recommendation here!" The dispensaries are more like recreational amusement shops than clinics for the sick, and the overall culture is one of "Here's a sweet loophole" partying more than anything else.[58]

These arguments are supported by statistical data from states that have passed laws legalizing marijuana for medical purposes. The great majority of people who have received state approval to buy and use medicinal pot are not seeking relief from cancer, AIDS, multiple sclerosis (MS), or other serious diseases. Instead, most patients who apply for medical marijuana cards merely cite "chronic pain" or "severe pain" in the paperwork they submit to state authorities in California, Colorado, Michigan, Oregon, and elsewhere. Ferguson explains:

> No one doubts that medical marijuana has brought relief to [Colorado's] cancer patients, AIDS sufferers and MS victims. But these aren't the customers the state is really serving. At the beginning of [2010], Colorado health department records show that only 2 percent of registered patients had cancer; 1 percent had HIV/AIDS. There were 94 percent who suffered "severe pain"—a catchall condition that can be entirely subjective and difficult for a doctor to measure or verify.[59]

Even some advocates of medical marijuana have urged authorities to tighten up regulations on who can qualify for medicinal pot. In California, which in 1996 became the first state to legalize medical marijuana when voters passed Proposition 215, influential supporters of that initiative like Scott Imler now complain that "most of the dispensaries operating in California are little more than dope dealers with store fronts."[60] In 2012 Kevin A. Sabet, who directs the Drug Policy Institute at the University of Florida and ranks as one of the nation's most influential antilegalization voices, described the medical marijuana scene in California as shockingly corrupted:

> Most Californians know that "medical" marijuana has become a sad joke. . . . A recent study found that the average Prop 215 card holder was a 32-year-old white male

with no life threatening illness (instead they got pot for indications such as "relaxation") and a history of alcohol and drug use. The typical scene of a "dispensary" involves 300-pound bouncers guarding tinted doors, inside of which are 21-year-old kids giving medical advice and medicine called "Purple Haze" to anyone with a pulse. Homicides, increased youth drug use, property and neighborhood crime and advertising to kids have all become a part of doing business. Today's dispensaries—really pot shops selling the drug under the guise of medicine—bear little resemblance to voters' intent.[61]

A medical marijuana clinic in California is open for business. One critic of California's law says that "most of the dispensaries operating in California are little more than dope dealers with store fronts."

Marijuana Use in the Workplace

Another flashpoint in the debate over medical marijuana concerns workplace safety and performance. Many companies have a zero-tolerance policy toward drug use and make clean drug tests a condition of employment. In these situations even people who are using pot legally can be fired. Advocates of medical marijuana legalization assert that states should revise their disability discrimination laws so that people who choose legally available pot as their medication are not threatened with the loss of employment.

Critics of medical marijuana flatly reject such assertions as foolish and unsafe. They charge that changing the laws would force many employers to keep marijuana-using workers on the job even if they are visibly impaired and unable to perform their duties safely and effectively. Insurance experts have urged companies to maintain a no-tolerance policy toward marijuana use, even for medical considerations. "If a forklift driver who uses [medical marijuana] is involved in an accident and hurts someone, you're on the hook" for a potential lawsuit, explains one insurance executive to business owners. "The risk associated with allowing a worker with medical marijuana in [his/her] system to stay at work is not a risk I would endorse taking."[62]

Insurance industry agents and experts have assured business owners that as long as federal law prohibits medical marijuana, they will not get in legal trouble for firing employees even if they are armed with state marijuana cards. "Marijuana, no matter what state law says, is still illegal under federal law," says one labor law attorney, "so employers would be well-served to prohibit all drugs that are illegal under state and federal law."[63]

Another option that is sometimes mentioned is to place employees with state-issued medical marijuana cards on disability leave or on temporary leave under provisions of the federal Family and Medical Leave Act. This approach gives workers time to find other employment or explore other ways of relieving their pain or other symptoms of illness.

Conducting Medicine by Popular Vote

Antilegalization groups have expressed considerable frustration with the manner in which medical marijuana has been legalized in many states. They feel that it is a big mistake to place important medical and health-care decisions on state or local ballots. After all, most voters do not have any medical training or deep familiarity with the medicinal properties of marijuana. Opponents of medical marijuana believe that any changes in the legal status of marijuana should be left to the administrators and researchers of the FDA. "The ballot initiative–led laws create an atmosphere of medicine by popular vote, rather than the rigorous scientific and medical process that all medicines must undergo," complains the antilegalization group Drug Free America Foundation. "[The FDA's] uniform and reliable system of drug approval and regulation . . . is being intentionally undermined by . . . medical marijuana initiatives."

Quoted in Mark Eddy. *Medical Marijuana: Review and Analysis of Federal and State Policies*. Washington, DC: Congressional Research Service, April 2, 2010, p. 43.

Legalization opponents believe that legalizing medical marijuana through ballot initiatives is wrong because the public is largely misinformed on the subject.

Worries About Stoned Driving

Some critics of medical marijuana legalization have issued grave warnings that the increased acceptance of medicinal pot will make the nation's roadways more dangerous. They assert that stoned drivers are just as dangerous as drunk drivers, and they predict that medical marijuana states will eventually see an upsurge in accidents and deaths due to people operating motor vehicles while high on medical cannabis.

CLAIMING A LINK BETWEEN LEGALIZATION AND ADDICTION

"Since legalization of marijuana for medical or general use would increase marijuana use rather than reduce it and would lead to increased rates of addiction to marijuana among youth and adults, legalizing marijuana is not a smart public health or public safety strategy for any state or for our nation."—Robert L. DuPont, president of the Institute for Behavior and Health

Robert L. DuPont. "Why We Should Not Legalize Marijuana." CNBC, April 20, 2010. www.cnbc.com/id/36267223.

Studies of driving fatalities have not yet substantiated this claim. In fact, a study of marijuana use and traffic deaths based on federal data from 1990 to 2009 found that states that have legalized medical marijuana experience lower numbers of fatal car accidents—perhaps because people in those states are smoking marijuana *instead* of drinking alcohol. "Driving under the influence of marijuana seems to be less risky because people who are high tend to be aware that they are impaired and compensate, while alcohol tends to increase recklessness and create false confidence," explains journalist Maia Szalavitz. "Also, people are more likely to smoke weed at home or in private, rather than out at bars or other public events that require driving to get to."[64]

Groups opposed to medical marijuana, however, are certain that the worst is yet to come. They believe that legalization of medicinal pot sends the wrong message to younger drivers, who might come to believe that there is little difference between

The subject of driving while under the influence of medical marijuana has become a hot-button issue in the legalization debate.

smoking marijuana and taking a couple of aspirin. They worry that this attitude, combined with increased access to pot in medical marijuana states, will eventually unleash a wave of dangerously impaired drivers on American roads.

Antilegalization groups also point to a 2012 review of international research on the risks of stoned driving. This review, published in the medical journal *BMJ*, suggested that driving after smoking marijuana might almost double the risk of involvement in a serious or fatal automobile accident. According to Robert L. DuPont, president of the anti–medical marijuana Institute for Behavior and Health, research is increasingly exposing "the terrible carnage out there on the roads caused by marijuana."[65] Opponents of legalization have thus joined with some U.S. law enforcement authorities and public officials in calling for laws making it illegal for people to drive with *any* trace of marijuana in their systems.

CHAPTER 5

MEDICAL MARIJUANA IN THE TWENTY-FIRST CENTURY

Medical marijuana advocates believe that the ballot victories of the 2012 election season represent the leading edge of a political and social surge that will soon make recreational and medical marijuana use legal across the entire United States. Opponents of legalization concede that the pro-marijuana camp has seized the momentum, but they insist that they can still ward off widespread legalization of the drug. Both defenders and critics of medical cannabis agree, however, that if pot ever becomes widely legalized for medicinal purposes, it is much more likely to be approved for recreational use, like alcohol and tobacco.

Shifting Political Winds for Medical Marijuana

As of early 2014 voters or legislators in seventeen states had passed laws in support of medical marijuana. Another eleven states— Alabama, Florida, Illinois, Iowa, Kansas, Kentucky, Maryland, Missouri, New Hampshire, New York, and West Virginia—were considering legislation that would legalize medical cannabis.

Supporters of these efforts predict that most states will pass laws legalizing medical marijuana within the next few years. "There's been a sea change" in public attitudes about pot, says Earl Blumenauer, a Democratic representative from Oregon who has long supported legalization. Blumenauer stated in 2013, "I'm absolutely convinced that in the next four or five years, [marijuana's] going to pass the point of no return"[66] and be regulated in much the same way as alcohol.

The confidence of marijuana legalization supporters stems not only from recent ballot box successes but from national public opinion polls that show support for legalizing medical pot consistently above the 50 percent level. Demographic trends may further boost public support for legalization in years to come. The fiercest opponents of marijuana legalization in the United States are senior citizens, whereas the most enthusiastic supporters of legalization are teenagers and people in their twenties. Many analysts believe that as elderly opponents die and teen supporters reach the age where they can exercise their voting rights, public support for medical marijuana—and marijuana legalization in general—will continue to increase.

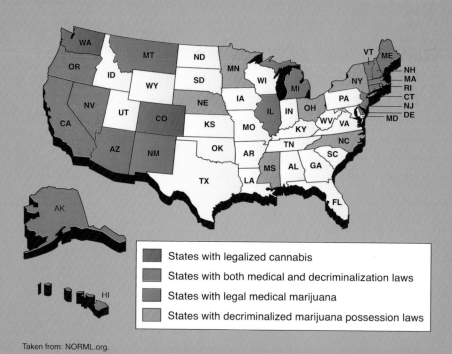

Marijuana Laws in the United States, 2013

- ■ States with legalized cannabis
- ■ States with both medical and decriminalization laws
- ■ States with legal medical marijuana
- ■ States with decriminalized marijuana possession laws

Taken from: NORML.org.

Republican congressman from California Dana Rohrabacher introduced a bill in the U.S. House of Representatives called the Respect State Marijuana Laws Act. Rohrabacher's bill sidesteps the medical and law enforcement debates about pot and simply states that legalization should be decided on a state-by-state basis.

Republicans have historically maintained a unified stance against any relaxation of America's marijuana laws. For decades, they rejected calls from liberal lawmakers to legalize medical marijuana. They have also opposed reductions in legal penalties for marijuana use and possession and resisted efforts to reclassify marijuana under the Controlled Substances Act so as to encourage additional scientific research on the plant. As journalist Josh Harkinson wrote in 2013, "Until recently, Republicans who supported ending pot prohibition were about as common as unicorns."[67]

The rise in public support for legalizing both medical and recreational marijuana, however, has prompted some conservative Republicans to reconsider their position on the issue. In early 2013, for example, conservative California representative Dana Rohrabacher introduced a bill in the U.S. House of Representatives called the Respect State Marijuana Laws Act.

Rohrabacher's bill sidesteps the medical and law enforcement debates about pot and simply states that legalization should be decided on a state-by-state basis. "It's a pragmatic approach that can appeal to individuals who, regardless of their view as to whether marijuana should be legalized, believe states should be allowed to determine their own marijuana policies,"[68] Rohrabacher stated.

The Quest for Total Legalization

Some medical marijuana advocates say that they will not rest until marijuana is legal for all adults for any kind of use. Colorado attorney Robert J. Corry Jr., who was a leading figure in that state's pot legalization campaigns, explains:

> Until it's legal for everyone—for recreational, spiritual, for any purpose—the patients are always going to get caught up in this mentality of "you're not really a legitimate patient, you're faking it, you're lying about your medical condition just so that you can get marijuana." They're also going to get caught up in this unique-to-marijuana principle that you can only have what is medically necessary. There is no other medicine or commodity that has that. You can have forty kegs of beer sitting in your garage and no one is going to say that you have [an unlawfully] excessive amount of alcohol, or you could have a hundred Oxy-Contin, the amount that can kill six horses, sitting in your medicine cabinet and nobody is going to say you've got an excessive amount. Until it's legal for everyone, the patients are never going to be safe because they'll be caught up in this netherworld.[69]

The pro-legalization camp is confident that the recent wave of laws approving medical marijuana will sway Americans to their position on pot. "Growing numbers of people will become familiar with cannabis and its derivative products," writes noted Harvard University psychiatrist Lester Grinspoon. "They will learn that its harmfulness has been greatly exaggerated and its usefulness underestimated. We can expect that with this growing sophistication about cannabis, there is likely to be mounting

Changes in Medical Marijuana Laws Around the World

Around the globe, the legality of medical marijuana varies greatly from nation to nation. The general trend, however, is toward policies that legalize medical cannabis. Nations that have made it legal for physicians to prescribe medical marijuana for patients include Austria, Canada, Finland, Germany, Israel, Italy, Netherlands, and Portugal.

Some countries are even moving toward complete legalization of marijua-na, including Israel, Belgium, Netherlands, and the Czech Republic. In addition, several nations in Latin America, which is traditionally the source of much of the world's marijuana crop, are considering legalizing marijuana. Political leaders in Guatemala, Mexico, and Uruguay have all endorsed legalization as a way to reduce the influence of violent drug gangs within their borders.

Hemp plants are harvested from a greenhouse in Netherlands. Netherlands has joined Austria, Canada, Germany, Finland, Israel, and Portugal in legalizing medical marijuana.

pressure to change the way we as a society deal with people who use this drug for any reason."[70]

Antilegalization Groups Vow to Fight On

Opponents of marijuana legalization admit that most recent ballot battles have not gone their way. They even acknowledge that medical marijuana will almost certainly increase in popularity over the short term, especially if states that have approved medical marijuana clean up some of their more confusing and contradictory regulations about the drug. However, antilegalization groups insist that the pro-legalization crowd is declaring victory prematurely.

Some critics of medical marijuana believe that as marijuana use increases, their warnings about marijuana use will be proved true. They charge that as legalization spreads, it will unleash miseries—higher rates of lung cancer, increased carnage on

Nationally and internationally, opponents of medical marijuana's legalization vow to fight on, as this protest in Brazil shows.

roadways, spikes in the use of heroin and other drugs—that may reawaken the nation to marijuana's dangers.

Opponents also emphasize that although states around the country have passed legislative acts and ballot measures legalizing medical marijuana, national marijuana laws have not budged. "At the federal level, it's still 1985," writes journalist Andrew Ferguson. "Marijuana retains its status as a Schedule 1 controlled substance, the legal equivalent of heroin and LSD, with 'a high potential for abuse' and 'no currently accepted medical use.' That designation sharply limits the medical research that can be done with marijuana."[71]

THE CLAWS AND TEETH OF MARIJUANA PROHIBITION

"Progress is being made against Marijuana Prohibition. Soon, this modern-day Prohibition will be as extinct as a saber tooth tiger. In the meantime, however, that cornered tiger still has sharp claws and long teeth that can destroy human life and freedom."—Pro-legalization activist and attorney Robert J. Corry Jr.

Robert J. Corry Jr. "The Audacity of Dope: Obama Breaks Medical Marijuana Promise." *The Blog, Huffington Post,* October 11, 2010. www.huffingtonpost.com/robert-j-corry-jr /wont-get-fooled-again-oba_b_758389.html.

Congress has the power to change marijuana's legal status, but political observers do not expect any such action in the near term. They say that many lawmakers in Washington remain leery of supporting such a change out of fear that they will be labeled "soft on crime" by political opponents. At least for the next several years, then, federal marijuana policy will likely depend to a great degree on the attitude and policy priorities of Barack Obama and his successors. For example, if the next president directs government agencies to end prosecutions of medical cannabis businesses or expresses support for state-level ballot measures to legalize medical pot, the medical marijuana movement will continue to build momentum.

Racial Disparities in Enforcement of Marijuana Laws

In 2013 the American Civil Liberties Union (ACLU) released a study of arrest rates for marijuana possession across the United States. The organization reported that in every region of the country, blacks are arrested much more often than are whites, even though their rates of usage are about the same. Overall, the ACLU reported that blacks are 3.73 times as likely as whites to be arrested for marijuana possession.

One reason for this disparity may be that in recent years, marijuana laws have been loosened primarily in areas of the country with large white populations. But the ACLU and other observers believe that racial bias is the primary factor behind the higher arrest rates for African Americans. They point out, for example, that black arrest rates for marijuana possession were far higher than white arrest rates in every single one of the twenty-five most populated counties in the United States in 2010. In half a dozen of those counties, the arrest rate was more than four times higher for blacks than whites, despite roughly equal rates of usage.

The American Civil Liberties Union reports that blacks are 3.73 times more likely than whites to be arrested for marijuana possession.

On the other hand, the next presidential administration could also use federal law enforcement agencies to push back against states that have legalized marijuana for medicinal or recreational use. "The DEA can raid state-legal pot shops, as it has done with medical marijuana dispensaries," writes journalist Jacob Sullum. "The Justice Department can use asset forfeiture as an intimidation tactic against landlords and threaten banks that accept deposits from pot businesses with money laundering charges. The IRS [Internal Revenue Service] can make life difficult for pot sellers by disallowing their business expenses."[72]

Unlocking the Chemical Secrets of Marijuana

The future of medical marijuana in the United States will also be shaped by the research efforts of scientists, both in America and around the world. Although U.S. research into marijuana's effects on the mind and body have been severely limited by the plant's restricted legal status, American research laboratories like the University of California's Center for Medicinal Cannabis Research have nonetheless been able to conduct ongoing clinical trials to investigate the safety and effectiveness of marijuana in treating various ailments and illnesses. More extensive medical marijuana research is being conducted in other countries by government agencies, scientific organizations, and pharmaceutical companies.

These efforts could produce findings that will boost public and political support for medical marijuana. Some studies, for example, have already yielded promising indications that THC and other active ingredients in marijuana may be helpful in preventing degenerative brain diseases like Alzheimer's. Other researchers say that they are developing strains of marijuana with high levels of cannabidiol (CBD) that can ease the discomfort of arthritis and other types of chronic pain. Opponents of legalizing medical marijuana, meanwhile, are urging scientists to go beyond just pursuing studies on marijuana's health benefits. They also want researchers to fully investigate potential health hazards that might be associated with prolonged marijuana usage, such as increased vulnerability to depression or abuse of harder drugs.

The University of California's Center for Medicinal Cannabis Research released a report of ongoing clinical trials to investigate the safety and effectiveness of marijuana in treating various ailments and illnesses.

Finally, opponents and supporters of medical marijuana agree that the issue could be influenced in unpredictable ways by the development of synthetic versions of marijuana. Unlike marijuana, which is usually smoked, these synthetic drugs are being developed by pharmaceutical companies to be taken as a pill or spray, rather than inhaled. These medications are more likely to be approved for commercial sale by the FDA because their ingredients can be carefully measured, producing the same dosage time after time. The best-known drugs containing synthetic versions of THC and CBD that have thus far been developed are Marinol (taken in pill form) and Sativex (a mouth spray). Marinol is already being sold in the United States and Canada. Sativex is sold in Canada, Germany, the United Kingdom, and several other countries, and observers expect it will eventually gain FDA approval.

THE WISDOM OF FDA TESTING

"Usually, drugs have to pass exacting testing by the Food and Drug Administration before they go on the market. There's a good reason for this: we don't want people spending money on products that might be ineffective or actually harmful."—Journalist and political commentator Charles Lane

Charles Lane. "Medical Marijuana Is an Insult to Our Intelligence." *PostPartisan* (blog), *Washington Post*, October 20, 2009. http://voices.washingtonpost.com/postpartisan/2009/10/medical_marijuana_is_an_insult.html.

Some observers believe that these synthetic versions of marijuana will eliminate any excuse that Americans have for using the marijuana plant for medicinal purposes. "The moment that Sativex goes on the market [in the United States], the need for medical dispensaries, caregivers, and growers—and all the confusions and prevarications that attend them—disappears,"[73] declares Ferguson.

Others, however, do not believe that the arrival of synthetic marijuana products will slow the present trend toward full legalization of the marijuana plant, whether for medical or recreational use. "People in this country have been exposed to misinformation about marijuana their entire lives," says Paul Armentano, who serves as deputy director of the National Organization for

Working to reform marijuana laws

Home   About NORML   About Marijuana   State Info   Legal Issues   Library   News Releases   Blog

Study: "There Is Now Clear Evidence That Cannabinoids Are Useful For The Treatment Of Various Medical Conditions"
Scientific findings from over 100 controlled clinical trials

Do your part to
HELP LEGA

JOIN

ACT!

NORML NEW
Sign up to rec
analysis from

Name

Legalization   Doctors & Patients   Busted?   Research   Lawyers

Criminal marijuana prohibition is a failure. Over 20 million Americans have been arrested for marijuana offenses since 1965. NORML believes that the time has come to amend criminal prohibition and replace it with a system of legalization, taxation, regulation, and education

support for legalization

WRITE TO CONGRESS»

The National Organization for the Reform of Marijuana Laws website (shown) offers information on the therapeutic benefits of medical marijuana.

the Reform of Marijuana Laws. "[But] government is . . . coming to understand that prohibition fails and regulations works. They see that in recent years tobacco and alcohol use have dropped to historic lows, not from prohibition but controls and regulations. We should apply that approach to marijuana."[74]

NOTES

Introduction: The Debate Over Medical Marijuana

1. Institute of Medicine. *Marijuana as Medicine? The Science Behind the Controversy*. Washington, DC: National Academy of Sciences, 2000, pp. 3–4. www.nap.edu/openbook.php ?record_id=9586&page=3.

Chapter 1: The History of Medical Marijuana

2. Quoted in Michael Aldrich. "History of Therapeutic Cannabis." In *Cannabis in Medical Practice: A Legal, Historical, and Pharmaceutical Overview of the Therapeutic Use of Marijuana*, edited by Mary Lynn Mathre. Jefferson, NC: McFarland, 1997, p. 36.

3. Aldrich. "History of Therapeutic Cannabis," p. 38.

4. Quoted in Aldrich. "History of Therapeutic Cannabis," p. 40.

5. Martin A. Lee. *Smoke Signals: A Social History of Marijuana—Medical, Recreational, and Scientific*. New York: Scribner, 2012, pp. 20–21.

6. Lee. *Smoke Signals*, p. 26.

7. Lee. *Smoke Signals*, p. 37.

8. Quoted in Greg Campbell. *Pot, Inc.: Inside Medical Marijuana, America's Most Outlaw Industry*. New York: Sterling, 2012, p. 54.

9. Quoted in Rudolph Joseph Gerber. *Legalizing Marijuana: Drug Policy Reform and Prohibition Politics*. Westport, CT: Greenwood, 2004, p. 9.

10. Quoted in Richard J. Bonnie and Charles H. Whitebread. *The Marijuana Conviction: A History of Marijuana Prohibition in the United States*. New York: Lindesmith, 1999, p. 117.

11. Quoted in Larry Sloman. *Reefer Madness*. New York: St. Martin's Griffin, 1998, p. 76.

12. Jacob Sullum. "The War over Weed: If You Know Why Marijuana Was Banned, You Know Why It Should Be Legalized." *Reason*, January 2013, p. 60.

13. Wendy Chapkis and Richard J. Webb. *Dying to Get High: Marijuana as Medicine*. New York: New York University Press, 2008, p. 29.

14. Quoted in Andrew Ferguson. "The United States of Amerijuana." *Time*, November 11, 2010. www.time.com/time /magazine/article/0,9171,2030925,00.html.

15. Institute of Medicine. *Marijuana and Medicine: Assessing the Science Base*. Washington, DC: National Academies Press, 1999, p. 3.

16. Matt Labash. "Gone to Pot: The Medical Marijuana Charade." *Weekly Standard*, October 11, 2010. www.weeklystandard .com/articles/gone-pot.

17. Ferguson. "The United States of Amerijuana."

18. Campbell. *Pot, Inc.*, pp. xii–xiii.

19. Quoted in Campbell. *Pot, Inc.*, p. xiv.

20. Quoted in Mike Riggs. "Obama Administration Overrides 2009 Ogden Memo, Declares Open Season on Pot Shops in States Where Medical Marijuana Is Legal." *Hit & Run* (blog), *Reason*, June 30, 2011. http://reason.com/blog/2011/06/30 /white-house-overrides-2009-mem.

21. *Economist*. "Up in Smoke: Marijuana Laws," April 14, 2012. www.economist.com/node/21552609.

Chapter 2: How Medical Marijuana Works

22. Institute of Medicine. *Marijuana and Medicine*, pp. 4–5.

23. GSC Cannabis Laboratories. "Cannabis Sativa and Indica Compared." December 7, 2011. http://gsccannabislab.blog spot.com.

24. National Cannabis Prevention and Information Centre. "Cannabinoids," October 1, 2011. http://ncpic.org.au/work force/alcohol-and-other-drug-workers/cannabis-information /factsheets/article/cannabinoids.

25. Hash, Marihuana & Hemp Museum. "The Biochemistry of Cannabis." http://hashmuseum.com/the-biochemistry-of -cannabis.

26. Americans for Safe Access. *Chronic Pain and Medical Cannabis*. Washington, DC: ASA, 2011, pp. 7–8.

27. Hash, Marihuana & Hemp Museum. "Medicinal Applications of Cannabis." http://hashmuseum.com/medicinal-applications-of-cannabis.

28. Labash. "Gone to Pot."

Chapter 3: The Benefits of Legalizing Medical Marijuana

29. American College of Physicians. *Supporting Research into the Therapeutic Role of Marijuana*. Philadelphia: ACP, 2008, p. 1.

30. Mark Eddy. *Medical Marijuana: Review and Analysis of Federal and State Policies*. Washington, DC: Congressional Research Service, April 2, 2010, p. 46.

31. Jerome Kassirer. "Federal Foolishness and Marijuana." *New England Journal of Medicine*, January 30, 1997, pp. 366–367.

32. Quoted in Americans for Safe Access. "Medical Cannabis Endorsements." http://americansforsafeaccess.org/downloads/Medical%20Cannabis%20Endorsements.pdf.

33. Quoted in Americans for Safe Access. *Chronic Pain and Medical Cannabis*, p. 16.

34. Eddy. *Medical Marijuana*, p. 30.

35. Eddy. *Medical Marijuana*, p. 28.

36. Lee. *Smoke Signals*, p. 291.

37. Lee. *Smoke Signals*, p. 291.

38. Chapkis and Webb. *Dying to Get High*, pp. 115–116.

39. Anthony Cotton. "On the Defensive: Marijuana Law Should Go Up in Smoke." *Wisconsin Law Journal*, December 19, 2012. http://wislawjournal.com/2012/12/19/on-the-defensive-marijuana-law-should-go-up-in-smoke.

40. Greg Campbell. "8 Myths About Marijuana: There Is No 'Safe Dosage' of Marijuana." *Huffington Post*, April 18, 2012. www.huffingtonpost.com/greg-campbell/marijuana-myths_b_1434718.html#s882036&title=There_is_no.

41. Quoted in Chapkis and Webb. *Dying to Get High*, pp. 120–121.

42. Lee, *Smoke Signals*, p. 173.

43. Quoted in Chapkis and Webb. *Dying to Get High*, p. 173.

44. Institute of Medicine. *Marijuana and Medicine*, p. 6.

45. James Austin. "The Decriminalization Movement." NORML, 2005, p. 4. http://norml.org/pdf_files/NORML_Rethinking _Decriminalizing_Marijuana.pdf.

46. Karen O'Keefe and Mitch Earleywine. *Marijuana Use by Young People: The Impact of State Medical Marijuana Laws.* Marijuana Policy Project, 2011. www.mpp.org/reports/teen -use.html.

47. Campbell. *Pot, Inc.*, p. 199.

48. Quoted in Donovan X. Ramsey. "Race, Politics, and the Battle to Legalize Marijuana." Grio, January 26, 2013. http:// thegrio.com/2013/01/26/race-politics-and-the-battle-to -legalize-marijuana.

Chapter 4: The Drawbacks of Legalizing Medical Marijuana

49. Quoted in Eddy. *Medical Marijuana*, p. 26.

50. American Society of Addiction Medicine. "Public Policy Statement on Medical Marijuana," April 12, 2010. www .asam.org/advocacy/find-a-policy-statement/view-policy -statement/public-policy-statements/2011/12/15/medical -marijuana.

51. Barry McCaffrey. "We Are on a Perilous Path." *Newsweek*, February 3, 1997, p. 27.

52. American Society of Addiction Medicine. "Public Policy Statement on Medical Marijuana."

53. Ferguson. "The United States of Amerijuana."

54. US Drug Enforcement Administration. *The DEA Position on Marijuana*, January 2011, p. 31. www.justice.gov/dea/pr /multimedia-library/marijuana_position.pdf.

55. Quoted in US General Accounting Office. *Marijuana: Early Experiences with Four States' Laws That Allow Use for Medical Purposes.* Washington, DC: GAO, November 2002, p. 36.

56. Quoted in Albert T. Johnston. *Medical Marijuana and Marijuana Use.* New York: Nova Science, 2009, p. 67.

57. Quoted in Peter Hecht. "Oakland Pot Tax Adds Fuel to Legalization Fire." *Sacramento Bee*, August 3, 2009. Reproduced at http://www.420magazine.com/forums/international-cannabis-news/98749-oakland-pot-tax-adds-fuel-legalization-fire.html.

58. Brett McCracken. "Should Christians Smoke Medical Marijuana? No—It's a Bad Witness." *Christianity Today*, June 2011, p. 62.

59. Ferguson. "The United States of Amerijuana."

60. Quoted in Kevin A. Sabet. "Medical Marijuana: Buyers' Remorse in California Reaches New Heights." *Huffington Post*, July 25, 2012. www.huffingtonpost.com/kevin-a-sabet-phd/medical-marijuana-buyers-_b_1704230.html.

61. Sabet. "Medical Marijuana."

62. Quoted in Chad Hemenway. "Courts: Employers Have No Duty to Keep Medical Marijuana Users." *National Underwriter Property & Casualty Insurance*, March 28, 2011, p. 19.

63. Quoted in Diane Cadrain. "The Marijuana Exception: People Who Use Marijuana for Medical Conditions, as Permitted in 14 States and Washington, D.C., May Be Shielded from Prosecution—but Employers Can Still Enforce Zero-Tolerance Policies." *HRMagazine*, November 2010, p. 40.

64. Maia Szalavitz. "Why Medical Marijuana Laws Reduce Traffic Deaths." *Time*, December 2, 2011. http://healthland.time.com/2011/12/02/why-medical-marijuana-laws-reduce-traffic-deaths.

65. Quoted in Kristen Wyatt. "New Wrinkle in Pot Debate: Stoned Driving." MPR News, March 19, 2012. http://minnesota.publicradio.org/display/web/2012/03/18/stoned-driving.

Chapter 5: Medical Marijuana in the Twenty-First Century

66. Quoted in Matt Taylor. "Yes We Cannabis: The Legalization Movement Plots Its Next 4 Years." *Atlantic*, March 27, 2013. www.theatlantic.com/politics/archive/2013/03/yes-we-cannabis-the-legalization-movement-plots-its-next-4|-years/274356.

67. Josh Harkinson. "A GOP Bill to End the War on Pot." *Mother Jones*, April 20, 2013. www.motherjones.com/mojo /2013/04/republican-bill-could-end-war-pot-dana-rohra bacher.

68. Quoted in Harkinson. "A GOP Bill to End the War on Pot."

69. Quoted in Campbell. *Pot, Inc.*, p. 199.

70. Lester Grinspoon. Foreword to *The Pot Book: A Complete Guide to Cannabis—Its Role in Medicine, Politics, Science, and Culture*, edited by Julie Holland. Rochester, VT: Park Street, 2010, p. xxiii.

71. Ferguson. "The United States of Amerijuana."

72. Sullum. "The War over Weed," p. 60.

73. Ferguson. "The United States of Amerijuana."

74. Quoted in Ramsey. "Race, Politics, and the Battle to Legalize Marijuana."

Chapter 1: The History of Medical Marijuana

1. What is hemp, and where did it contribute to the growth in cultivation of marijuana?

2. How did racial attitudes influence the development of marijuana laws in America in the early twentieth century?

3. What are three factors that contributed to increased interest in medical marijuana in the second half of the twentieth century?

Chapter 2: How Medical Marijuana Works

1. What are the two main types of medical cannabis, and how do they differ from one another?

2. What are the most recognized chemical compounds, or cannabinoids, in marijuana?

3. What are three medical conditions for which marijuana has been discussed as a therapeutic tool?

Chapter 3: The Benefits of Legalizing Medical Marijuana

1. Provide three reasons why some medical marijuana advocates prefer natural marijuana over synthetic strains of cannabis.

2. Cite three reasons why medical marijuana advocates believe that the drug is safe to use.

3. Supporters of legalization say that it would bring a number of important social and economic benefits. List three of these purported benefits.

Chapter 4: The Drawbacks of
Legalizing Medical Marijuana

1. Describe three of the main health objections to medical marijuana.

2. What are the chief concerns about the misuse of medical marijuana?

3. Summarize the main concerns of critics about medical marijuana in the workplace.

Chapter 5: Medical Marijuana in the
Twenty-First Century

1. Why are medical marijuana advocates so confident that the drug will eventually be legalized throughout the United States?

2. Explain why marijuana's continued classification as a Schedule I controlled substance is so important.

3. Discuss the ways in which synthetic forms of marijuana could alter the debate over medical marijuana.

ORGANIZATIONS TO CONTACT

Americans for Safe Access (ASA)
1806 Vernon St. NW
Washington, DC 20009
Phone: (202) 857-4272
Fax: (202) 618-6977
Website: www.americansforsafeaccess.org

The ASA is an organization of patients, medical professionals, scientists, and concerned citizens that works to promote safe and legal access to medical marijuana through public education and advocacy programs.

Community Anti-Drug Coalitions of America (CADCA)
625 Slaters Ln., Ste. 300
Alexandria, VA 22314
Phone: (800) 542-2322
Fax: (703) 706-0565
Website: www.cadca.org

CADCA is a national network of organizations dedicated to keeping their communities safe, healthy, and free of drugs. It has adopted a position of opposition to legalizing medical marijuana.

Drug Free America Foundation (DFAF)
5999 Central Ave., Ste. 301
St. Petersburg, FL 33710
Phone: (727) 828-0211
Fax: (727) 828-0212
Website: www.dfaf.org

The DFAF is dedicated to supporting and promoting policies that reduce illegal drug use and drug addiction. This organization is firmly opposed to legalizing medical marijuana, citing a variety of medical and societal concerns.

Drug Policy Alliance
DPA Office of National Affairs
925 Fifteenth St. NW, 2nd Fl.
Washington, DC 20005
Phone: (202) 683-2030
Fax: (202) 216-0803
Website: www.drugpolicy.org

The Drug Policy Alliance is an organization dedicated to promoting drug policies that are grounded in science and compassion. The group's active lobbying and public education efforts to reform state and federal drug policies include promotion of marijuana as a safe and valuable medical resource.

Marijuana Policy Project (MPP)
236 Massachusetts Ave. NE, Ste. 400
Washington, DC 20002
Phone: (202) 462-5747
Website: www.mpp.org

The MPP focuses on supporting state and federal legislation aimed at legalizing marijuana and replacing it with a system of regulation and control. Its website also serves as an information clearinghouse for all marijuana-related subjects, including medical marijuana.

**National Organization for the Reform
of Marijuana Laws (NORML)**
1600 K St. NW
Mezzanine Level
Washington, DC 20006-2832
Phone: (202) 483-5500
Fax: (202) 483-0057
Website: www.norml.org

Founded in 1970, NORML has for more than forty years been at the forefront of efforts to legalize marijuana for recreational, medical, industrial, and other uses. Its website contains a wide range of information on marijuana laws and legalization efforts across the country.

Books

Julie Holland, ed. *The Pot Book: A Complete Guide to Cannabis— Its Role in Medicine, Politics, Science, and Culture*. Rochester, VT: Park Street, 2010. This book provides a broad but accessible overview of the history of marijuana in American society, medicine, and law.

Martin A. Lee. *Smoke Signals: A Social History of Marijuana— Medical, Recreational, and Scientific*. New York: Scribner, 2012. This book provides a look at the changing fortunes of marijuana and those who use it over time in America from a perspective that is generally sympathetic to the legalization movement.

Internet Sources

Tim Dickinson. "Obama's War on Pot." *Rolling Stone*, February 16, 2012. www.rollingstone.com/politics/news/obamas-war -on-pot-20120216. This feature story published by music and culture magazine *Rolling Stone* (a strong proponent of marijuana legalization) criticizes the Obama administration for its marijuana policies.

Mark Eddy. *Medical Marijuana: Review and Analysis of Federal and State Policies*. Washington, DC: Congressional Research Service, April 2, 2010. www.fas.org/sgp/crs/misc/RL33211 .pdf. Although this research report by the highly respected and nonpartisan Congressional Research Service does not reflect 2012's wave of medical marijuana legalization, it nonetheless provides a clear and objective primer on the arguments for and against medical cannabis.

Frontline. "The Pot Republic." Video, 2011. www.pbs.org/wgbh /pages/frontline/the-pot-republic. This Public Broadcasting System webpage provides the full video of an investigative report on medical marijuana that was broadcast in 2011 by the *Frontline* news program, as well as maps, interviews, and other features related to the issue.

Matt Labash. "Gone to Pot: The Medical Marijuana Charade." *Weekly Standard*, October 11, 2010. www.weeklystandard.com /articles/gone-pot. This article criticizes the medical marijuana movement as a cynical and transparent attempt to legalize pot for recreational use.

PBS NewsHour. "Clearing the Smoke: The Benefits, Limits of Medical Marijuana." Video, August 23, 2011. http://video .pbs.org/video/2103797319. This ten-minute video provides a good overview of the medical marijuana issue, explaining the positions of both supporters and opponents.

Donovan X. Ramsey. "Race, Politics, and the Battle to Legalize Marijuana." Grio, January 26, 2013. http://thegrio.com /2013/01/26/race-politics-and-the-battle-to-legalize-marijuana. This article examines the marijuana legalization issue by discussing the impact of current marijuana laws on black and Hispanic communities.

Kevin A. Sabet. "Medical Marijuana: Buyers' Remorse in California Reaches New Heights." *Huffington Post*, July 25, 2012. www.huffingtonpost.com/kevin-a-sabet-phd/medical-mari juana-buyers-_b_1704230.html. This article by an opponent of legalization describes California's decision to legalize medical marijuana as an unmitigated disaster.

Websites

"Archive," National Public Radio (www.npr.org/templates /archives/archive.php?thingId=131327322). This website's medical marijuana archive provides links to all news stories on medical marijuana broadcast over National Public Radio since 2010.

INDEX

PICTURE CREDITS

ABOUT THE AUTHOR

Kevin Hillstrom is an independent scholar who has written numerous books on environmental and social issues, U.S. politics and policy, and American history.